W9-AQU-203

MAR 1974

RECEIVED
OHIO DOMINICAN
COLLEGE LIBRARY
COLUMBUS, OHIO
43219

The Poems of
THOMAS HARDY

The Poems of
THOMAS HARDY
A Critical Introduction

by
KENNETH MARSDEN

New York
OXFORD UNIVERSITY PRESS
1969

© KENNETH MARSDEN 1969

ACKNOWLEDGEMENTS

Quotations from *The Collected Poems of Thomas Hardy*, Copyright 1925 by The Macmillan Company, are reprinted with permission of The Macmillan Company; permission is separately granted to reprint from the same volume 'Life and Death at Sunrise', 'Snow in the Suburbs', 'Waiting Both', Copyright 1925 by The Macmillan Company renewed 1953 by Lloyds Bank Ltd, and 'Proud Songsters', Copyright 1938 by Florence E. Hardy and Sydney E. Cockerell renewed 1956 by Lloyds Bank Ltd.

Quotations from the manuscipt of *Wessex Poems* reprinted with permission of the Museum and Art Gallery Committee of the Corporation of Birmingham.

'At Max Gate' from *Collected Poems 1908–1956* by Siegfried Sassoon reprinted with permission of George Sassoon.

821.89
H272 Ma
1969

PRINTED IN GREAT BRITAIN

This book is dedicated to
my chief supports during its
writing
Professor Barbara Hardy
and
My Wife, Rosalind

89647

39647

FOREWORD

THIS account of Hardy's poetry is a revised version of a study originally approved for a higher degree of the University of London. Despite its academic origin it is at least as much an introduction as a work of research. I have, with one exception, used only published sources, but have tried to anchor the conclusions by quotation and close reference. There were two starting points; the peculiarity of Hardy's present reputation, and his use of language. Early drafts of Chapters 1 and 7 were, therefore, the earliest portions and the rest of the work arose naturally from these twin centres.

The reader will find that I attach considerable importance to Hardy's philosophy though I make no attempt to discuss it systematically. Both too much and too little attention has been given to it by commentators. Too much because many accounts consider it in almost complete isolation from Hardy's creative work; and too little because inadequate attention has been focused on how it affected the bulk of his verse and not merely a few overtly 'philosophical' pieces. I have therefore, when consulting commentators, taken as my guides those, such as Rutland and Webster, who stay closest to Hardy and his life, and have avoided the systematizers.

Hardy is, in my opinion, a very personal poet; an understanding and appreciation of his poetic persona is the most satisfactory approach to the poetry. This is not a contradiction, but a reinforcement of the remarks about the importance of the philosophy. 'Character' and 'Philosophy' moulded each other and re-acted upon each other and the poetry is a compound formed by the two. There are no short cuts to understanding and appreciation; neither concentration upon a few 'select' poems nor the attempt to find one all-inclusive pattern will get the reader to the heart of the poems. The general and the local must be taken together and their point of meeting is the poetic persona which created the poems and is manifested in them.

The anomalous critical standing of Hardy's verse was my starting point, as it was that of other critics of Hardy, notably Hynes and Guerard. My use of, and citations from, critics has consequently been extensive but selective; the views of Blackmur, Blunden, Hynes and Southworth, in particular, have been considered frequently. My debt to Dr Hynes is considerable. His book has been a constant inspiration and I should not like my disagreements, sometimes fundamental, with him to hide my gratitude, or the enlightenment gained by testing my conclusions against his. (I ought also to point out that all my comments on Mr Southworth's work refer to the original edition. The Preface to the second edition, New York 1966, shows that he has modified some of his views and sees more merit in Hardy's verse than he did.)

Professor Purdy's bibliography and Dr Hickson's study of versification are excellent examples of that type of scholarly work which can be fully appreciated only by those who have benefited from it. The fact that few surface signs are left of this benefit make it all the more important to record it as strongly as possible.

The omission of *The Dynasts* and *The Famous Tragedy of the Queen of Cornwall* arises from no intention to belittle further these under-estimated works. *The Dynasts* seems to attract writers interested only in philosophy and a serious consideration of its literary merits is long overdue. But it was clear that any attempt at discussion on the same terms as the shorter poems would result in serious distortion of *The Dynasts* itself; and even having a slightly misleading title seemed better than that.

My thanks are due to Professor Barbara Hardy for the most valuable form of assistance; encouragement during periods when months passed without any progress at all. The manuscript benefited greatly from the scrutiny of Dr Harold Brooks and would probably have gained more if I had had sufficient wisdom to adopt more of his suggestions. Mr Basil Greenslade gave some valuable advice and Miss Eleanor Robertson earned my gratitude by some exemplary typing.

Finally I must thank the officers of The Athlone Press for their patience in dealing with a rather careless author.

K.M.

Ongar, Essex
4 April 1968

CONTENTS

ACKNOWLEDGEMENTS

Quotation throughout this volume from *The Collected Poems of Thomas Hardy* is made by kind permission of The Trustees of The Hardy Estate, Macmillan and Company Ltd, The Macmillan Company of Canada Ltd, and The Macmillan Company, New York. 'At Max Gate' from *Collected Poems 1908–1956* by Siegfried Sassoon is quoted by kind permission of George Sassoon.

Acknowledgement is also due to the Museum and Art Gallery Committee of the Corporation of Birmingham for permission to quote from the manuscript of *Wessex Poems*.

I

Introduction

> . . . and by this time Thomas Hardy, the actual father of
> modern verse in England, was writing his poems . . .
>
> (Geoffrey Grigson)

It might be expected that on the basis of such a recommend-
ation Hardy would be an acknowledged master of poetry,
the subject of frequent tributes, critiques, analyses and
discussions. The tributes are, it is true, numerous and from
varied sources:

> [Dylan Thomas] would spend hours talking about, and reading
> aloud, the poems of Hardy as he gobbled shell-fish and washed
> them down with bottled beer. (John Davenport)

> Not long ago Mr Robert Graves declared that, of twentieth-
> century poets, the best influences for younger writers were
> Thomas Hardy and Robert Frost. (Cecil Day Lewis)

> No one has taught me anything about writing since Thomas
> Hardy died. (Ezra Pound)

What is surprising is that none of these tributes is anything
more than that; they are not expanded into anything more
substantial. We are, indeed, frequently given no further
information at all. Dylan Thomas, for instance, never says,
to the best of my knowledge, why 'Hardy was his favourite
poet of the century'.[1] Extended criticism is rare and often

---

[1] Vernon Watkins in Dylan Thomas, *Letters to Vernon Watkins*, ed.
Vernon Watkins (London, 1957), p. 17.

carping, even though there is plenty of approval too. Hardy seems to resemble the semi-mythical character of whom it was said that he had no enemies, but that all his friends disliked him.

The general public appears to be more favourable since *The Collected Poems of Thomas Hardy* has been frequently reprinted since its first publication in 1919. Most of these volumes must, however, remain unread since it is rare in my experience to meet anyone who has first-hand knowledge of the book, though it is easy to find acquaintance with popular anthologies, whose compilers seem to copy languidly from each other, for instance 'Weathers', 'The Darkling Thrush', 'In Time of the Breaking of Nations'.

When the critics become more specific the most surprising discrepancies are found. Dr Leavis believes that Hardy's reputation as a great poet 'rests upon a dozen poems',[1] Edmund Blunden seems to approve of about two hundred;[2] while R. P. Blackmur states that Hardy's rate of success with one common type of poem is about one in ten, which would give about one hundred for the whole corpus.[3] There is hardly more agreement about individual poems. J. Middleton Murry and Dr Leavis single out 'Neutral Tones' as a great poem, but G. M. Young refers to it as 'a copy of verses, nothing more'.[4] Dr Samuel Hynes has a low opinion of 'Timing Her': '. . . . a slack and awkward piece which

---

[1] F. R. Leavis, *New Bearings in English Poetry* (new edition) (London, 1950), p. 59.

[2] Edmund Blunden, *Thomas Hardy* (London, 1941), p. 249. Cited as Blunden.

[3] R. P. Blackmur, *Language as Gesture* (London, 1954), p. 74. Cited as Blackmur.

[4] *Selected Poems of Thomas Hardy*, ed. G. M. Young (London, 1940), p. xii. Cited as Young.

suggests that Hardy was not equal to the demands of the verse form'.[1] Sir Arthur Quiller-Couch, however, quotes it 'merely to show how this poet whose metrical muscles were hard and stiff at fifty odd . . . worked them supple, so that now the verse cadences to the feeling'.[2] J. G. Southworth says of 'Near Lanivet 1872': 'This rather weak, ineffective and prosy poem . . . versifying an anecdotal experience that has been insufficiently subjected to the powers of imagination'.[3] Read and Dobrée, however, selected this poem for their anthology and Professor Dobrée many years later confirmed his high opinion of it. Hynes refers to 'A Singer Asleep' as 'a weak, conventional elegy' (p. 22), but Blackmur classes it as a success 'ending with a magnificently appropriate image' (p. 75).

This list, which could be extended, is surprising in itself, but becomes much more so when we remember that it is drawn not from a small body of verse (in which case the critics would be forced to discuss the same poems), but from over 900 poems; often to exemplify specific qualities. Disagreement among critics is normal, but this seems excessive. It is perhaps more than coincidence (since there are many resemblances between the two poets) that Wordsworth offers the closest parallel.

. . . making the usual complaints to me . . . of Mr Wordsworth's minor poems: I admitted that there were some few of the tales and incidents in which I could not myself find a sufficient cause

---

[1] Samuel Hynes, *The Pattern of Hardy's Poetry* (Chapel Hill, 1961), p. 85. Cited as Hynes.

[2] Sir Arthur Quiller-Couch, *Studies in Literature* (first series) (Cambridge, 1918), p. 198.

[3] James Granville Southworth, *The Poetry of Thomas Hardy* (New York, 1947), p. 51. Cited as Southworth.

for their having been recorded in metre. I mentioned the 'Alice Fell' as an instance; 'Nay,' replied my friend . . . 'I cannot agree with you *there*!—that, I own *does* seem to me a remarkably pleasing poem.' In the *Lyrical Ballads* . . . I have heard at different times, and from different individuals, every single poem extolled and reprobated . . .'[1]

Another peculiarity is the haste of all the critics to assure us that Hardy wrote a great deal of inferior verse. One becomes so used to this that it is easy to forget that it is not normal. Wordsworth and Tennyson, for instance, are not usually treated like this; and to argue that Time has done the critic's 'sieving' for him in their case leaves unexplained the fact that Yeats's critics spend little, if any, time informing their readers that the *Wanderings of Oisin* and *The Shadowy Waters* are trivial and tedious. It appears, therefore, that Hardy's reputation far from being reasonably fixed, is fluid, anomalous and uncertain. He is a poet whose work is widely purchased, but seldom read; frequently mentioned, but rarely examined; regarded as masterly, but often denigrated. He is generally admitted to have considerable merit, but there is little agreement as to where it is to be found.

Hynes remarks that 'the difficulties which lie in the way of liking Hardy are numerous, and are both in the verse and outside it' (pp. 3–4). The difficulties in the verse, which are ultimately the only important ones, will be considered later; to deal with the external difficulties first seems to be logical. It involves describing, however briefly, the critical ambience in which Hardy's poetry has had to exist.

[1] S. T. Coleridge, *Biographia Literaria*, ed. J. Shawcross (Oxford, 1907), p. 54.

2

Hardy began publication seriously as a poet in the 1890s. There were a number of poets in favour with various sections of the public at this time, but none of them seemed to have much in common with him. Housman, who re-sembles him in some ways, became popular, but he ob-viously had a far more immediate appeal; and, in any case, paid for the first edition of *A Shropshire Lad* himself.

The trouble was that although Hardy's reputation as a novelist was probably useful in drawing attention to his poems, it was an obstacle to appreciation. There appears to be a partly unconscious reluctance to take seriously any extension of an established reputation into a new field.

Almost all the fault finding was, in fact, based on the one great antecedent conclusion that an author who has published prose first, and that largely, must necessarily express himself badly in verse. . . .

In the present case, although it was shown that many of the verses had been written before their author dreamed of novels, the critics' view was little affected that he had 'at the eleventh hour', as they untruly put it, taken up a hitherto uncared-for art.[1]

As the second quotation shows, Hardy had to face a further difficulty; that what was really a life-long interest seemed to be an old-age hobby or dilettante work. These attitudes eventually vanished in all reputable critics, except possibly T. S. Eliot,[2] but are still active, sometimes in

[1] Florence Emily Hardy, *The Later Years of Thomas Hardy* (London, 1930), pp. 76, 77. Cited as *Later Years.*

[2] 'I am willing to pay due respect, for instance, to the poetry of George Meredith, of Thomas Hardy, of D. H. Lawrence as part of their œuvre, without conceding that it is as good as it might have been had they chosen

B

disguised forms ('I didn't know he wrote all those poems'), among the wider public.

Furthmore, as Hynes points out, he was handicapped by the *kind* of reputation he had gained (p. 17). Some of the poems showed the same pre-occupation as *Tess of the D'Urbervilles* and *Jude the Obscure* and were therefore judged as a metrical extension of them. Despite Hardy's hope of avoiding trouble by writing in verse ('If Galileo had said in verse that the world moved, the Inquisition might have let him alone', *Later Years*, p. 58), attacks upon his philosophy continued throughout his life. It is probable that disappointed expectation played its part too; there was good scenic description and comic dialogue in the novels; therefore they ought to appear in the verse. These attitudes gradually faded, but at one time they were very strong. The first edition of Duffin[1] does not discuss the poems at all, while Child[2] regards them as very minor satellites of *The Dynasts*. W. R. Rutland, as late as 1938, wrote that 'the poetry is in the nature of a commentary on the novels'.[3]

The first people to have been in key with Hardy's verse were men who were young in the 1914–18 period (among others, Sassoon, Blunden, Graves, C. H. Sorley,[4] I. A. Richards). They plainly felt closer emotional kinship with him than most earlier, or later, readers did. Unfortunately

to dedicate their whole lives to that form of art.' T. S. Eliot, *A Choice of Kipling's Verse* (London, 1941), p. 5.

[1] H. C. Duffin, *Thomas Hardy, A Study of the Wessex Novels* (Manchester, 1916).

[2] Harold Child, *Thomas Hardy* (London, 1916).

[3] W. R. Rutland, *Thomas Hardy. A Study of his Writings and their Background* (Oxford, 1938), p. 264. Cited as Rutland.

[4] Sorley, killed in 1915, is the first good poet to show the influence of Hardy, e.g. 'A Hundred Thousand Million Mites We Go', obviously inspired by *The Dynasts*.

this produced no extended criticism (Blunden's book belongs to a later period). More recent opinion (e.g. Blackmur, Hynes, Southworth) does take the verse seriously, but tends to be over-severe and rather carping.

What can be called, without prejudice to future discussion, Hardy's 'philosophy' is relevant here. Generally speaking, the early critics and those later ones, such as Rutland, who were temperamentally in agreement with them, tended to regard his outlook as perverse and gloomy. The next generation are much more sympathetic, though this usually has to be deduced from casual remarks and the fact that they wanted to visit him.[1] Later critics revert partly to the earlier attitude, but their position tends to be based on the belief that the philosophy is a nuisance and inartistic, or rather anti-artistic since it is thought to be inhibiting or distorting.

Another obstacle which is largely outside the verse is the shifts in literary values which have taken place in the last forty years. These are hard to describe and almost any statement is likely to be disputed, but one of their characteristics is a prejudice against minor poetry; that is, poetry which is not, and usually does not pretend to be, of comparable merit to the outstanding examples of the particular genre. This seems to be a prejudice of critics; poets are, I think, less affected.[2] One immediate result is that for much

[1] 'Since the war began I had taken to reading Hardy and he was now my main admiration among living writers. . . .' Siegfried Sassoon, *Siegfried's Journey* (London, 1945), p. 13 (cited as Sassoon). This book has many references to Hardy which show the strong impression he made, e.g. pp. 45, 64, 70, 75, 79–80, 88–93, 147–50, 169, 177, 181, 193. Sassoon visited Hardy at this time, as did Graves and Blunden.

[2] According to Vernon Watkins, Dylan Thomas liked Hardy the best of this century's poets in spite of realising that Yeats was the greatest of them.

of this century a good deal of competent verse which would have been read and liked in earlier ages has been attacked or ignored; competence, particularly if exhibited in one of the traditional forms, often fails to earn any respect, though it is frequently demanded as a *sine qua non*. Randall Jarrell puts the point effectively enough:

It is hard to write even a competent naturalistic story, and when you have written it what happens?—someone calls it a competent naturalistic story. Write another 'Horatian Ode', and you will be praised as one of the finest of our minor poets. No, as anyone can see, it is hardly worthwhile being a writer unless you can be a great one; better not sell your soul to the Muse till she has shown you the critical articles of 2100.[1]

Much of Hardy's work exists at rather low tension and there are few 'knock out' successes; he is a poet whom the reader must allow to grow on him. This kind of poetry has not found much critical favour in the last forty years. The tendency has been to downgrade any work which is not equal to the poet's best. Here is an example from a good critic of Hardy:

> If It's Ever Spring Again
> (Song)
>
> If it's ever spring again,
>   Spring again,
> I shall go where went I when
> Down the moor-cock splashed, and hen,
> Seeing me not, amid their flounder,
> Standing with my arm around her;

Philip Larkin records this in the Preface to *The North Ship* (2nd ed. London, 1966), p. 10.

[1] *Poetry and the Age* (London, 1955), p. 75.

If it's ever spring again,
      Spring again,
I shall go where went I then.

If it's ever summer-time,
      Summer-time,
With the hay crop at the prime,
And the cuckoos—two—in rhyme,
As they used to be, or seemed to,
We shall do as long we've dreamed to,
If it's ever summer-time,
      Summer-time
With the hay, and bees achime.[1]

Hynes comments as follows:

One can immediately point to a number of technical flaws in this poem: the multiple and awkward inversions and the comic *flounder–around her* rhyme in the first stanza, the padding in the second (there is no point to the parenthetical *two* in the thirteenth line or in the last three words of the fourteenth, and the final line is entirely filler). Cuckoos rhyme and bees chime to make the rhyme scheme, not because rhyming and chiming are natural to them. The device of repetition is overworked and ineffective; the last lines of the stanzas in particular are feeble as refrains.

(pp. 69–70)

Hynes goes on to say that the poem's 'fundamental failure is a failure of tension'; that the poem is based upon a *then-now* contrast, but since the *now* 'has no existence in the poem itself' there is no real contrast. 'The nostalgia which suffuses the poem has no clear origin, and so remains gratuitous and sentimental'. He then proceeds to compare the poem unfavourably with 'Bereft'.

[1] *Collected Poems of Thomas Hardy* (London, 1962), p. 563 Cited as *Collected Poems*.

To take the last point first; the inferiority of the poem to 'Bereft' is obvious, but I think it probable that this valid assessment is responsible for most of the rest of the critique, which is much less well founded. Hynes has allowed the *relative* inferiority of this poem to blind him to what kind of poem it is and consequently to misinterpret quite a number of details. He is, in fact, treating it much too seriously. Although he notes that it is a memory poem, does not have a true 'antinomial' structure and is lacking in tension, he fails to see that the poem is comparatively light-hearted (Hardy is not usually so cheerful). To anyone who realises this, the 'flounder-around her' rhyme need cause no trouble; nor need the inversions, since I can see no sign of any strong emotion, actual or intended. The 'two' seems meaningful enough if Hardy is thinking of one particular occasion or group of occasions (and he frequently is), especially when it is accompanied by the 'or seemed to'. Hynes falls foul of this also, failing to see that it forms a semi-ironic commentary on the 'two', casting a little doubt on the memory picture; 'there always *seemed* to be two answering each other, but . . . .'

Cuckoos rhyme and bees are achime because the cuckoos answer each other and the bees make a regular monotonous sound, which is one of the normal meanings of 'chime'. If it is maintained that, nevertheless, the need for rhyme caused the choice of these particular words, I cannot see why this is *in itself* a fault.

This is not a particularly weak poem; it is, however, an unfashionable one, and the treatment it receives from a fairly sympathetic critic, is typical of a great deal of Hardy criticism, often of better poems.

There are at least two subsidiary reasons why critical

opinion has tended to be undecided and often cool. The first is the form of Hardy's poetic output; a huge 'epic drama', a 'play for mummers' and 922 poems are not the kind of thing which raises initial enthusiasm in the intending reader. Nor are some of Hardy's recorded literary comments; for instance:

'Why!' he said, 'I have never in my life taken more than three, or perhaps four, drafts for a poem. I am afraid of it losing its freshness.'

'Oh, but I admire the *Iliad* greatly. Why, it's in the *Marmion* class!'

'All we can do is to write on the old themes in the old styles, but try to do a little better than those who went before us.'[1]

If these offences to the sophisticated were unknown, ignored or condoned, there were the obstacles raised by his friends to be surmounted. In the long run his reputation as an inspirer of modern poetry has not been to his advantage, since it has aroused expectations of a great innovator, which must be largely disappointed. As we shall see later it is more fruitful to think of Hardy as being at the end of a tradition rather than at the beginning of a new era; G. M. Young recognized this, and his deep knowledge of the Victorian period ought to give weight to his opinion.

It is plain that to sail successfully through so many critical currents needs a very 'tight' ship, and it is here that other problems begin. All these difficulties, serious though they are, will play a less and less important part as time goes on. It is the obstacles *in* the verse which are really important, and of these the most notorious is the 'philosophy.'

[1] Robert Graves, *Goodbye to All That* (London, 1929), pp. 374, 376, 377.

II

Philosophy

BEFORE Hardy's philosophy can be considered a preliminary problem has to be solved; whether the philosophy exists. Although Hardy wavered on this point, publicly at any rate, he usually denied that it did; his position, roughly, was that he had philosophical views, but no Philosophical View. Practically every preface to his poems that he wrote takes this attitude.

> I also repeat what I have often stated on such occasions, that no harmonious philosophy is attempted in these pages—or in any bygone pages of mine, for that matter.
>
> *Winter Words* (*Collected Poems*, p. 796)

And to take an early example:

> Unadjusted impressions have their value, and the road to a true philosophy of life seems to lie in humbly recording diverse readings of its phenomena as they are forced upon us by chance and change.
>
> *Poems of the Past and the Present* (*Collected Poems*, p. 75)

Furthermore, he could point to some poem which was opposed to whatever metaphysical or moral sin he was accused of:

> ... notwithstanding the surprises to which I could treat my critics by uncovering a place here and there to them in the volume. *Winter Words* (*Collected Poems*, p. 795)

Put so, his position seems logically impregnable. The difficulty is that it affronts the common sense and experience of every reader. To begin with, there are a number of poems which must be intended to put forth philosophical beliefs and concepts. Usually they have a metaphorical or narrative structure, but this seldom obscures the purpose, which is to make some view explicit. Poems such as 'A Sign Seeker', 'An Inquiry', 'The Subalterns', 'The Bedridden Peasant', 'The Lacking Sense', 'God-Forgotten' and 'Agnosto Theo' must be of this kind if they are to mean anything at all.

In addition, there are a number of anecdote poems which appear too simple to be taken at face value; 'The Dame of Athelhall', 'The Pedestrian', 'The Enemy's Portrait', 'A Wife Comes Back' for instance. The reader, with the patently philosophical poems in his memory, finds it hard to believe that these anecdotes are not illustrative of a general thesis—corroborative detail intended to give artistic verisimilitude to an otherwise bald and unconvincing theory. This view may be wrong; it can hardly be unreasonable, though Hardy seemed to think that it was.

The writers who have treated Hardy from a philosophic angle appear, then, to have some justification, though they have made the philosophy far more elaborate and formal than Hardy probably ever intended it to be; the more 'literary' critics, on the other hand, have not treated it seriously enough. He himself remarked that he was not a trained philosopher ('though I do read *Mind* occasionally') and the best accounts occur in letters:

. . . that the said Cause [of things] is neither moral nor immoral but *un*moral: 'loveless and hateless' I have called it, 'which neither good nor evil knows'—etc., etc. (*Later Years*, p. 217)

I have the commonplace feeling that the Timeless Reality knows no difference between what we call good and what we call evil, which are only apparent to the consciousness of organic nature generally—which consciousness is a sort of unanticipated accident.

(Letter to J. Mc. E. McTaggart quoted Blunden, p. 229)

There was nothing new or striking in such views; the germ of them can be found in Pascal, and they had been put forward explicitly, though in semi-fictitious clothing, before Hardy's birth:

To me the Universe was all void of Life, of Purpose, of Volition, even of Hostility; it was one huge, dead, immeasurable, Steam-Engine, rolling on, in its dead indifference, to grind me limb from limb.   (Carlyle, *Sartor Resartus* Book II Chap. vii)

Later it was put equally forcibly by a writer with a very different background and upbringing from either Carlyle or Hardy:

It [the Universe] . . . evolved itself out of a chaos of scraps of iron and behold!—it knits. I am horrified at the horrible work and stand appalled. I feel it ought to embroider, but it goes on knitting. . . . The infamous thing has made itself: made itself without thought, without conscience, without foresight, without eyes, without heart. It is a tragic accident—and it has happened. You can't interfere with it. It knits us in and it knits us out. It has knitted time, space, pain, death, corruption, despair, and all the illusions,—and nothing matters.[1]

At the end of the century Elie Metchnikoff, one of its greatest and most painstaking scientists, committed him-

[1]Joseph Conrad in a letter dated 20 Dec. 1897 to R. B. Cunninghame Graham in G. Jean-Aubry, *Joseph Conrad: Life and Letters* (London, 1927), p. 216.

self to the belief that Mankind at any rate was an accident:
'Man is a kind of miscarriage of an ape . . .'

An example earlier than any of these, a sonnet written in
1815, is particularly interesting because the author, Cole-
ridge, did not hold this opinion, but realised that it was a
logical alternative to belief in Immortality.

Human Life
On the Denial of Immortality

If dead, we cease to be; if total gloom
   Swallow up life's brief flash for aye, we fare
As summer-gusts, of sudden birth and doom,
   Whose sound and motion not alone declare,
But are their whole of being! If the breath
   Be Life itself, and not its task and tent,
If ever a soul like Milton's can know death;
   O Man! thou vessel purposeless, unmeant,
Yet drone-hive strange of phantom purposes!
   Surplus of Nature's dread activity,
Which, as she gazed on some nigh-finished vase,
Retreating slow, with meditative pause,
   She formed with restless hands unconsciously.
Blank accident! nothing's anomaly!

This is the driving force behind the 'philosophy'; that the
Universe was non-sentient, a kind of machine; that con-
sciousness was an accident and a misfortune as well. Most of
the quirks, obsessions and insights for which Hardy is
famous, the mechanical imagery, the peculiar home-made
mythology, the trivial incidents, the fascination with the
workings of Chance, and much else besides, could be logic-
ally derived from this 'core' (which does not imply that
Hardy did so derive them in *every* case).

Although this view, or something like it, could have been

held at any time, it only seems to have seeped into the consciousness of the general educated public about the middle of the nineteenth century. Even then its impact came with varying force and results; neither Conrad nor Metchnikoff, for instance, seems to have been greatly affected by it emotionally. For an account of what this view of the Cosmos *could* produce, we may turn to G. M. Young.

If I were asked what the total effect of Darwin, Mill, Huxley and Herbert Spencer upon their age had been, I should answer somehow thus. They made it difficult, almost to impossibility, for their younger contemporaries to retain the notion of a transcendent governing Providence. They forced the imagination of their time into a monistic habit of thought, of which *The Dynasts* is the great, and solitary, artistic record. To those who pass that way, the various devices with which believers of another sort reconcile Providence with Evil, or with Pain, will almost necessarily seem servile or sophistical. For them, there is nothing to reconcile; because to them, inherent in It, in the essence and operation of It, abides

'. . . the intolerable antilogy
Of making figments feel'

The injustice of uncompensated pain, the darkening of our hours of happiness by the thought that they too are passing towards Nothing, round these two themes Pessimism revolves in a closed circle. Men of an abundant active temperament will not often think of them: men absorbed in some intellectual pursuit have little time to think of them. But for the meditative man there is no escape and no consolation. . . . (pp. xviii–xix)

Nearly all this is worth careful consideration, particularly the remarks that 'Pessimism revolves in a closed circle' and that 'for the meditative man there is no escape . . . .', which contain much of the source of, and excuse for,

Hardy's obsessions and repetitions. There are good reasons for supposing that Hardy's temperament and upbringing were such as to cause him to be affected to an almost painful extent when 'the great storm broke' (Young, p. xviii).

The exact date and causes of Hardy's loss of Faith are uncertain since it fell between 1862 and 1867, the period of his life which is least known. He was working in London, young and obscure; and the only information which has survived is what he, a reticent man, allowed to survive. He had a conventional religious upbringing, describing himself late in life as 'churchy', and he matured late. H. C. Webster has assembled a number of examples and quotations tending to prove that far from it being true that 'He never expected much', he was a youth who expected too much.[1]

In addition, it seems likely that Hardy was exposed to a particularly strong blast of the 'great storm'. The writers mentioned by G. M. Young, together with *Essays and Reviews* (1860), were probably the *literary* sources of his loss of Faith. Leslie Stephen was not one of these pioneers (being, on the contrary, one of their products); nor was he responsible for Hardy's 'conversion' since they did not meet until 1873. Furthermore, they saw little of each other in later years. However, for a comparatively short period in the seventies the two seem to have been in close contact: '... the man whose philosophy was to influence his own for many years, indeed, more than that of any other contemporary, and received a welcome into his household, which was renewed from time to time ...'[2]

Stephen was not only an agnostic, but a propagandist for

[1] Harvey Curtis Webster, *On a Darkling Plain* (Chicago, 1947), pp. 25–6.
[2] Florence Emily Hardy, *The Early Life of Thomas Hardy* (London, 1928), p. 132. Cited as *Early Life*.

agnosticism, and was at this time heavily engaged in controversy. For tender material like Hardy to be brought into intimate contact with such a man was all that was needed to drive him even farther from his former moorings. That there was some special connection between them seems clear from the peculiar incident which took place in 1875.

One day (March 23rd 1875) I received from Stephen a mysterious note asking me to call in the evening, as late as I liked. I went and found him alone, wandering up and down his library in slippers . . . he said he wanted me to witness his signature to what, for a moment, I thought was his will, but which turned out to be a deed renunciatory of holy-orders under the act of 1870. (*Early Life*, p. 139)

Although this incident is well known its strangeness does not seem to have been appreciated.[1] Why should Stephen make a point of asking Hardy to do something which could have been performed by anyone capable of writing his own name, and be willing to wait for him? The simplest explanation seems to be that Stephen regarded Hardy as a kind of disciple and wanted him to play an acolyte's part in the ceremony. Hardy, in fact, remarks that 'Our conversation then turned on theologies decayed and defunct, the origin of things, the constitution of matter, the unreality of time, and kindred subjects' (*Early Life*, p. 139).

The effect of all this on a man of Hardy's meditative temperament must have been devasting.[2] He observed wryly that

[1] Rutland, p. 82, describes the incident as 'significant', but does not emphasize or comment upon it.

[2] Lionel Johnson applied to Hardy the words of Newman '. . . just the impatient sensitiveness which relieves itself by a definite delineation of

The originator of a depressing mental view, mood, or idea, is less permanently affected by its contemplation, than those who imbibe it from him at second hand. Jeremiah probably retired to rest at night and slept soundly long before the listeners to his fearful words closed their eyes. . . .[1]

This is dated the end of December 1873; that winter Hardy met Stephen for the first time.

2

Such was the philosophy and something of its general effect on the poet; some of its workings will be considered in more detail later. The present question is its effect upon the reader; which means, in fact, another question: 'Why is the philosophy unpopular?'

In the first place it is disliked—usually from a Christian standpoint—as philosophy. This feeling certainly motivated some of his early critics and readers, and one can detect a similar attitude in Rutland.

Secondly, when Hardy abandoned orthodox Christianity he abandoned the system of mythology and symbols which traditionally accompanies it, and substituted from time to time mythologies largely of his own invention, e.g. The Mother, King Doom, etc. Parallel to this is an interest in ghosts and the supernatural generally, surprising until one realizes that it is the natural result of the impact of a mechanistic philosophy on a fundamentally believing mind. Hardy himself appeared to be at least half-aware of this:

what is so hateful to it'. *Post Liminium: Essays and Critical Papers* (London, 1911), p. 145.

[1] *Thomas Hardy's Notebooks*, ed. Evelyn Hardy (London, 1955), pp. 44–5. Cited as *Notebooks*.

My nerves vibrate very readily; people say I am almost morbidly imaginative; my will to believe is perfect. If ever ghost wanted to manifest himself, I am the very man he should apply to. But no—the spirits don't seem to see it.[1]

The third reason is a feedback from the poems. Since a number of poems are poor and embody the philosophy in some way, the philosophy is held to be responsible for the badness and is therefore disliked. This conclusion then spreads a general hostility over the whole work.

A fourth factor is the assumption that the philosophy, a nineteenth-century view of the Cosmos, is now exploded. This is not true; the theory has become unfashionable, in literary circles at any rate, without ever having been refuted.[2] This factor is both the most pervasive and the most difficult to define, being part of the intellectual ambience rather than a crystallized opinion. Its presence can usually be detected when the critic, having stated that there is nothing wrong with the ideas in themselves, goes on under the tacit assumption that there is, lamenting that Hardy had such inferior intellectual sustenance. None of the dilemmas given in the quotation from Young above have been solved; they are usually ignored, often by people who would have been tormented by them if they had been living sixty or seventy years ago. If these ideas are dead, then they are of the kind that are dead but won't lie down. They can return to

[1] William Archer, *Real Conversations* (London, 1904), p. 37.

[2] It is, however, worth noting that in a recent book *Words in the Mind* (London, 1965), Charles Davy gives three assumptions as 'bound up with the current scientific world picture': (a) Matter must antedate Mind; (b) Life rose out of dead matter; (c) The Universe is a kind of vast dynamic machine with no meaning or purpose in any human sense. Davy says that these are unproved and unprovable, but does not claim that they are superficial or implausible (p. 111).

disturb and nag, and it is probable that the peace of mind of many people is maintained only by *refusing*, often unconsciously, to think about them. (The beginning of Eliot's *The Waste Land* gives a classic account of a similar condition.)

The contrast with Yeats, for instance, is very marked. His poetry, much of which depends on concepts far more fantastic than anything in Hardy, meets with far less opposition on philosophical grounds. Since few people are going to be disquietened by his religio-magical mish-mash, it and the poems embodying it can be examined coolly; its difficulties and improbabilities can be pointed out, but tribute paid at the same time to its undoubted efficiency as a structure for his verse.

All this tends to depress Hardy's reputation, so that a poet who meditates on Death, Chance, Destiny, Time, the concepts which have formed the substance of poetry throughout the ages, has his work described by one of the best critics of our time as '. . . a thicket of ideas, formulas, obsessions, undisciplined compulsions, nonce insights and specious particularities' (Blackmur, p. 52).

3

The core of Hardy's philosophy, as given in the letters to Noyes and McTaggart is tenable, even if it is not held firmly and explicitly by many people today. One important difference between this century and the last is that this particular interpretation of the universe does not now have the compelling, almost self-validating, power of creating conviction that it had then. There is considerable evidence to show that the 1870s was the time when mechanistic philosophy reached its height in intellectual standing.

c

A reading of a fair amount of the writing of the last forty years on the problem of Belief has left me convinced that it is capable of solution only at the personal level. That it can be solved there is plain enough; Lucretius, Dante and Milton still have readers. The two points which seem to provide the firmest footing are that the reader can in fact willingly suspend his disbelief, and that one reason why he can do this is that the good poet manifests a 'character' which helps to create trust and, therefore, belief; the second point goes at least as far back as Aristotle. The strength and essential honesty of Hardy's poetic persona is something which will be mentioned several times in this study. The main contention at present, however, is that he is entitled, if not to a willing suspension of disbelief, at least to a little preliminary goodwill. It is important that this goodwill should not be refused, because objections to the philosophy often merge imperceptibly into better-grounded objections to the manner and frequency of its expression.

Although there are several reasons for the narrowness and repetitiveness of Hardy's themes, the effect of the 'great storm' upon a meditative nature is probably as strong as any. It affected him like a personal sorrow and had the same nagging quality (the effect on more combative natures such as Stephen and John Morley was, of course, very different). Hardy underlined in his copy of Coleridge's poems the following lines from the Preface:

> ... the mind, *full of its late sufferings* ... *can endure no employment not in some measure connected with them.*[1]

---

[1] Evelyn Hardy, *Thomas Hardy: A Critical Biography* (London, 1954), p. 76 (cited as Evelyn Hardy). See also Lionel Johnson's quotation from Newman on pp. 18–19 above.

Closely associated with this is the charge that he is buried in gloom, 'an inverted Micawber waiting for something to turn down'. It is true that one does not need to read far to find insufficiently motivated disasters, Blows of Fate and Missed Opportunities. It has been frequently remarked that normal humanity calculates chances much better than Hardy, but he answered this kind of objection, admittedly in a slightly oblique manner:

> . . . as, in looking at a carpet, by following one colour a certain pattern is suggested, by following another colour, another; so in life the seer should watch that pattern amid general things which his idiosyncrasy moves him to observe, and describe that alone. This is quite accurately, a going to nature, yet the result is no mere photograph, but purely the product of the writer's own mind. (*Early Life*, p. 198)

The 'world' produced by Hardy is certainly a product of his own mind; but the contention that it has no reference to the world commonly observed is much less certain. The world to certain kinds of temperament is like that, and they cannot be proved wrong any more than their opponents can; so they are usually labelled 'Morbid'. Another or Hardy's underlinings from Coleridge's Preface was the reference to 'sleek favourites of fortune' who condemn all 'melancholy discontentedness' (Evelyn Hardy, p. 76).

Readers of William James's *The Varieties of Religious Experience* will be familiar with the distinction which he, following Francis Newman, makes between the Once Born and the Twice Born, and lectures IV and V, 'The Religion of Healthy-mindedness', give a vivid portrait of the type of temperament, the Once Born, which will have little time for Hardy.

The Twice Born, on the other hand, sees this world as 'a welter of futile doing.' This is something which the Once Born never learns and the Twice Born is sometimes obsessed by. As a result the two stare at each other in a silence broken from time to time by an exchange of insults. Hardy had his say in 'In Tenebris II':

> Their dawns bring lusty joys, it seems; their evenings
> all that is sweet;
> Our times are blessed times, they cry: Life shapes it
> as is most meet,
> And nothing is much the matter; there are many
> smiles to a tear;
> Then what is the matter is I, I say. Why should
> such a one be here?
>
> (*Collected Poems*, p. 154)

This poem is very bitter; the same point is made in a gentler fashion by 'The Impercipient' and also by a writer of greater philosophic accomplishment than Hardy: 'Job endured everything—until his friends came to comfort him; then he grew impatient.'[1]

It should be plain by now that Hardy's readers need a great deal of sympathy with him in both the original and common meanings of the word. His poetry is intensely personal; T. S. Eliot was undoubtedly right in singling him out as an outstanding modern example of personality in literature, which is, of course, another reason for a great deal of critical coolness. (The personality is that of the writer of the poems. It is not necessarily identical with that of Thomas Hardy, who was born near Dorchester in 1840, became an architect, wrote many novels, and so on. Mr

[1] Søren Kierkegaard, *The Journals* (Oxford, 1938), ed. A. Dru, p. 300.

J. I. M. Stewart's attempts to refute Eliot's accusations sometimes assume this identity.)[1]

A sympathetic critic of Hardy, the late F. L. Lucas, chose as an epigraph for his essay a quotation from Pascal:

On est tout étonné et ravi; car on s'attendait de voir un auteur et on trouve un homme.

When this happens it seems a little pedantic and graceless to insist that this is not quite what one came for!

4

Sympathy, then, is a necessity as Hardy himself emphasized:

It is the *unwilling mind* that stultifies the contemporary criticism of poetry. (*Later Years*, p. 184)

The understanding required is partly historical, an understanding of the spiritual plight in which Hardy found himself in his generation.

Just as in a case of herrings the top layer is crushed and spoilt and the fruit next to the crate is bruised and worthless, so too in every generation there are certain men who are on the outside and are made to suffer from the packing case, who only protect those who are in the middle. (Kierkegaard, p. 146)

It would be unwise to press the analogy very far, but Hardy was undoubtedly one of those on whom the packing case pressed hard. G. M. Young understood this very well and therefore his remarks on Hardy are of permanent value, though he showed a certain blindness to some of the more personal aspects of Hardy's work.

[1] 'The Integrity of Hardy' in *English Studies* 1948 (London, 1948), collected by F. P. Wilson. See especially p. 7.

The sympathy needed here merges slowly and impercep-
tibly into a more personal sympathy—into the ability to feel
with him. If one can do this, a large part of his work is
fine; if not, then it is difficult to avoid the carping tone
caused by lengthy contact with someone whose tempera-
ment clashes with one's own. If sympathy is achieved, then
one understands the remark quoted by Blackmur that
'Hardy's personal rhythm is the central problem in his
poetry' and Blackmur's own addition 'that once it has been
struck out in the open, it is felt as ever present' (p. 79).
(The 'ever' is very important; it goes part way towards
explaining why so much of Hardy's inferior verse can move
and grow on the reader.)

The essential thing is to remove all possible obstacles to
the perception of this rhythm. If we grasp the wanderings,
repetitions, and pressures which formed and tormented a
gifted individual, we see how the personal vision rises into
the common, how by speaking for himself he speaks for all.

The wind bloweth where it listeth, and the spirit of the age
may choose to speak, now in the accent of a rebel prince, as it did
when Byron filled Europe with his voice, and now in the tone of
an ageing man watching the fire die down and thinking of old
tunes, old memories. . . . But what we hear is the voice of an age,
of a generation carried beyond sight of its old landmarks, and
gazing doubtfully down an illimitable vista, of cosmic changes
endlessly proceeding and ephemeral suffering endlessly to be
renewed. (Young, pp. xxxii–xxxiii)

III

The Two Poets

ONE of the charges made against Hardy is that the bulk of his verse is monotonous and based on the repetition of a small stock of ideas. It is difficult to document this charge because it is rarely made in its pure form; usually exception is taken to what is said, as well as the frequency with which it is said. The following quotation is fairly typical:

One is apt to be discouraged by the frequency with which Mr Hardy has persuaded himself that a macabre subject is a poem in itself: that, if there be enough of death and the tomb in one's theme, it needs no translation into art, the bald statement of it being sufficient. (Rebecca West, *The Strange Necessity*, pp. 248–9)

It is clear that the same situation in different clothes occurs time and time again and is made more obvious by his arrangement of his verse. He placed next to each other poems which obviously were the result of the same inspiration and mere variations, as if in defiance of what anyone chose to think of them. An investigation into the nature and causes of this repetition may tell us something about the *kind* of poet Hardy is. The first thing to be noticed is that the condition, though acute in Hardy, is not unprecedented; Wordsworth has something to say on the matter:

The reader will find two poems on pictures of this bird among my poems. I will here observe that in a far greater number of instances than have been mentioned in these notes one poem has, as in this case, grown out of another, either because I felt that the subject had been inadequately treated or that the thoughts and images suggested in the course of composition have been such as I found interfered with the unity indispensable to every work of art, however humble in character.

(Note to 'Upon seeing a coloured drawing of a Bird of Paradise')

This seems a promising line of approach since a fair amount is known about Wordsworth's sources of inspiration and habits of composition.

In his book, *The Medium of Poetry* (1934), James Sutherland examined the inspiration and methods of two kinds of poet, taking Wordsworth as the type of the first and Keats of the second. The 'Wordsworths' have a number of fairly consistent characteristics in common.

INSPIRATION. This usually undergoes the following stages:

The poet has an experience; it may be something which happened to him personally (e.g. 'We are Seven') or was told to him (e.g. 'Lucy Gray').[1]

The experience lies more or less dormant for some time.

The memory of the experience is revived, and with it the emotion that accompanied the original experience.

Composition now begins.

Wordsworth is, of course, the classic case, but Browning has left a similar account of his own practice:

... An old peculiarity in my mental digestion—a long and obscure process. There comes up unexpectedly some subject for poetry which has been dormant, and apparently dead, for perhaps

[1] 'A Solitary Reaper' is a rather striking example; it *looks* like a personal memory but Dorothy Wordsworth seems to say that she and William knew of it only through their friend Wilkinson. *Journals of Dorothy Wordsworth* (London, 1941), ed. B. de Selincourt, i, 380.

dozens of years. A month since I wrote a poem of some two hundred lines [Donald] about a story which I heard more than forty years ago, and never dreamed of trying to repeat, wondering how it had so long escaped me; and so it has been with my best things.

Although Browning differed from Wordsworth in that, apparently, he sometimes thought of incidents as a subject for poetry quite early and they were, therefore, never completely dormant (for instance 'The Ring and the Book'), the general resemblance is very close. It is all the more striking in that Browning is not usually considered to have been inspired in the popular sense of the word and often wrote steadily in an almost 'Trollopian' manner.

FIDELITY. As the poem is grounded in a particular experience, there is a strong tendency for the details of that experience to persist in the finished poem. As Professor Sutherland points out, there was no need for Wordsworth to have dealt with the theme of 'We are Seven' in the way he did. He might have abandoned the incident entirely and written an 'Ode on the Inability of Childhood to comprehend the Idea of Dissolution'. Or, he could have used the same structure but abandoned the actual details (golden hair, porringer, etc.) and substituted others. In fact he rarely, in his earlier work, did either. This does not mean, of course, that he regarded all the details of the experience as on the same footing; he was anxious that *inessential* details should drop from memory.

He [believed to be Tennyson] took pains, Wordsworth said; he went out with his pencil and notebook, and jotted down whatever struck him most—a river rippling over the sands, a ruined tower on a rock above it, a promontory and a mountain and a mountain ash waving its red berries. He went home and wove the whole into a poetical description. . . .

. . . But Nature does not permit an inventory to be made of her charms! He should have left his pencil and notebook at home; fixed his eye as he walked, with a reverent attention on all that surrounded him, and taken all into a heart that all could understand and enjoy. Then, after several days had passed by, he should have interrogated his memory as to the scene. He would have discovered that while much of what he had admired was preserved to him, much was also most wisely obliterated. That which remained—the picture surviving in his mind—would have presented the ideal and essential truth of the scene, and done so in a large part by discarding much which, though in itself striking, was not characteristic.[1]

PRIMACY OF SUBJECT. The subject comes first both chronologically and artistically. It is both the starting point of the poem and the reason for its existence. The purpose of 'Alice Fell', for instance, is to tell the story and thereby assist the reader in gaining any experience and wisdom that can be obtained from it. (It was not written to show Wordsworth's skill, nor apparently because he felt he had to write it.) Everything else was subsidiary, and anything of the nature of decoration was particularly to be avoided.

CHARACTER. During his 'non-inspired' periods, probably most of the time, the poet is lying fallow and is 'just folks'. One consequence of this is a series of disillusioned pen pictures and anecdotes by observers and acquaintances; for instance, of Wordsworth:

> . . . rather a hard and a sensible worldly sort of man.
> (Lord Cockburn)

> A cold hard man with jaws like a crocodile. (Carlyle)

[1] Aubrey De Vere, *Essays chiefly on Poetry* (London, 1887), ii, 276-7.

> It struck me forcibly at the time, that he would be a capital
> hand to drive a hard bargain with a Welsh pig-driver at a
> fair.   (John Jones, a Welsh poet)

and of Browning:

> Who was that too exuberant financier?
>   (Lady at dinner party)

The 'Keats' type is very different.

INSPIRATION. There is not usually any period of lying
fallow. Composition normally follows quickly upon the
initiating experience, e.g. the Flower and Leaf sonnet. There
is no waiting for experience. The poet is a man who has
learned to control an elaborate instrument and is looking
for every opportunity to use it; he is a cloud of poetic
emotion and ability looking for a subject to condense upon.

FIDELITY. There need be no fidelity to the original ex-
perience; all he needs is a starting point. The result is that
the first draft of a poem sometimes shows fundamental
differences from the final one; there is also the feeling that
the final product is something of an accident; it might
easily have been different. Sutherland instances the 'Ode
to a Nightingale' and the 'Ode to Autumn' among other
examples (p. 64), but the point is that it is a common
procedure with Keats.

SUBJECT. This takes second place to treatment. Instead of
thinking of the thing to be expressed, he delights in his
powers of expression. He is *making* something rather than
communicating something.

CHARACTER. The poet himself, though he may be efficient
enough in practical matters, usually strikes observers as an
unusual personality; and he is frequently in the throes of

composition. If he is unable for any reason to write, he may feel depressed and ill.

I had become all in a Tremble from not having written anything of late—the sonnet overleaf did me some good. I slept the better last night for it—this Morning, however, I am nearly as bad again. (Keats)

I live under an everlasting restraint—Never relieved except when I am composing—so I will write away. (Keats)

My passions when once they were lighted up, raged like so many devils, till they got vent in rhyme; and then conning over my verses, like a spell, soothed all into quiet. (Burns)

. . . it comes over me in a kind of rage every now and then . . . and then, if I don't write to empty my mind, I go mad. (Byron)

The use of language by the two types tends to be different. 'Tends' is, I think, as far as one can go, as the whole matter is complicated and counter-currents are often found. The tendency is for the 'Wordsworths' to use clear, simple, unadorned language; the object seems to be to achieve transparency. One should look *through* language, not *at* it. The 'Keatses' tend to produce ornate, complicated language; it is to be examined and admired. There is often little else to be seen apart from it. It is usually the 'Wordsworths' who are considered as thinkers, not the 'Keatses'.

Needless to say, these are polar types and some poets evade the categories altogether. The young Wordsworth and the young Keats are the nearest approach to a pure type.[1]

[1] Browning, for instance, though often Wordsworthian in inspiration, was much less so as regards fidelity (e.g. the amusing conversation below, p. 35).

2

Examination of Hardy in terms of these categories shows that, though basically a 'Wordsworth', he exhibits a curious mingling of the two types and the nature of a great deal of his poetic output is determined by this.

INSPIRATION. Many of Hardy's poems seem to have been the result of a process similar to that which produced Wordsworth's. A large proportion are reminiscences, in one form or another, of his courtship in Cornwall in the 1870s and were written after the death of Emma Hardy. Other poems, however, have a like origin and Hardy was aware of this:

I believe it would be said by people who knew me well that I have a faculty (possibly not uncommon) for burying an emotion in my heart or brain for forty years, and exhuming it at the end of that time as fresh as when interred. For instance, the poem entitled 'The Breaking of Nations' [sic] contains a feeling that moved me in 1870, during the Franco-Prussian War, when I chanced to be looking at such an agricultural incident in Cornwall. But I did not write the verses till during the war with Germany of 1914, and onwards. Query: where was that sentiment hiding itself during more than forty years? (*Later Years*, p. 178)

To take only one volume, *Human Shows*: it is possible to find easily ten poems which had little connection with Emma Hardy, but which were, nevertheless, probably inspired by particular events in the distant past; 'Singing Lovers', 'Coming up Oxford Street', 'Snow in the Suburbs', 'A Light Snowfall after Frost', 'Music in a Snowy Street', 'The Pair He Saw Pass', 'Louie', 'The Harbour Bridge', 'Once at Swanage' and 'A Beauty's Soliloquy during her Honeymoon'.

It is not easy to trace Hardy's steps. He had no Dorothy Wordsworth to record his experiences in her journals and most of his own papers have been destroyed, but the publication of Emma Hardy's *Recollections* shows that, like Wordsworth, he could be inspired by a second-hand experience and that a good poem could result. Perhaps the most remarkable example is the background of 'After Wind and Rain', which had previously been assumed to be a reminiscence of Hardy's courtship at St Juliot. It is now clear that these scenes come from Emma's childhood, that her memoirs were the source, and that the poem is not even a versification of a simple description, but a new creation suggested by a series of scattered remarks.[1]

FIDELITY. It has already been noted that it is difficult to check many of the details in Hardy's poems, but that he followed a similar method to Wordsworth seems clear. The first step is to compare this quotation with the remarks by Wordsworth on pages 29–30.

But their principle [the Impressionist school of painting] is, as I understand it, that what you carry away with you from a scene is the true feature to grasp; or in other words, *what appeals to your own individual eye and heart in particular* amid much that does not so appeal, and which you therefore omit to record.

(*Early Life*, p. 241)

Then one should read the poems which concern Emma Hardy, *A Pair of Blue Eyes*, Emma Hardy's *Recollections*,

[1] It was possible to see much earlier that some of his inspiration probably came from this source. For instance, 'The Going', which Hardy dates 'Dec. 1912', introduces the red rocks and Emma's riding; at this time Hardy had not revisited Cornwall, but had read Emma's *Recollections* in which both are mentioned. This section of the *Recollections* was printed in *Early Life* (pp. 90–1).

and the extracts from Hardy's notebooks given in Florence
Hardy's biography; and notice how certain details recur,
for example Emma's riding, the rain storm on Beeny cliff,
the seals, the red rocks. There seems to be no doubt that
they *are* there in the poem because they *were* there in
actuality (they are not in themselves impressive; other details
as good or better could have been invented) and made their
impression, together with thousands which were forgotten.

('The poet takes note of nothing that he cannot feel
emotively', *Later Years*, p. 133.) This 'set' of Hardy's mind
is illustrated by the story of the conversation he had with
Browning.

> Hardy alluded to 'The Statue and the Bust' . . .; and observed
> that, looking at 'the empty shrine' opposite the figure of
> Ferdinand in the Piazza del' Annunziata, he had wondered where
> the bust had gone to, and had been informed by an officious
> waiter standing at a neighbouring door that he remembered
> seeing it in its place; after which he gave further interesting
> details about it, for which information he was gratefully rewarded.
> Browning smiled and said, 'I invented it'. (*Early Life*, pp. 261–2)

This possibility does not seem to have occurred to Hardy;
he would have taken a real bust as his starting point.

An example of apparently irrelevant detail is the rather
complicated framework of 'Leipzig'; the *existence* of the
framework was probably poetically necessary to Hardy (see
p. 90 below), but the *matter* leads to a rather obtrusive
explanation. I suspect that the German woman tambourine
player mentioned on page 164 of the *Early Life* had some-
how become associated in his mind with this story.

PRIMACY OF SUBJECT. Except in extreme cases, this is
likely to be a matter of how it strikes the reader, but one of

the symptoms is the accusation, sometimes justified, that what has been given is not a poem but the raw material for one— if it is not too trivial even for that. Most of Hardy's critics have, I think, felt the importance of subject, but have not realised it clearly because they were distracted by doubts about its validity or the frequency of its use. Ezra Pound is an exception:

> But he woke one to the extent of his own absorption in *subject* as contrasted with . . . 'treatment'.

> I do not believe there are more than two roads
>> (i) The old man's road (vide Tom Hardy)—CONTENT, the INSIDES, the subject matter.[1]

It may be significant that Pound has himself frequently been accused of obsession with subject matter. Arthur McDowall, an underestimated critic of Hardy, noted the paradox that although he seemed to be able to write on any subject, the subject was not indifferent, but on the contrary was very obtrusive.[2]

The theory of the primacy of subject can take extreme forms; some writers have held that close imitation is the way to achieve art and, sometimes, that the real incident is superior to *any* account of it. Wordsworth seems to have come near to this in the second edition of his Preface, and Hardy was a student of this manifesto ('which influenced me much'):

> Style—Consider the Wordsworthian dictum (the more perfectly the natural object is reproduced, the more truly poetic the picture). (*Early Life*, p. 190)

[1] *Letters of Ezra Pound* (London, 1951), ed. D. D. Paige, pp. 245, 332.
[2] Arthur McDowall, *Thomas Hardy, a Critical Study* (London, 1931), p. 217. Cited as McDowall.

Similar remarks can be found in the writings of Ezra Pound, D. H. Lawrence and Wallace Stevens. As illustration we have Hardy's defence of that ludicrous piece of versification, 'In the Days of the Crinoline'; ' "It was a true story," said Hardy eagerly' (Blunden, p. 247).

Poems such as 'The Contretemps', 'Her Second Husband hears her Story' and 'The Two Wives' obviously derive from the same conviction.

CHARACTER. Several visitors who were not overawed by Hardy's reputation have made some comment upon his ordinariness, e.g.

. . . and Mr Gosse has told me that, of all the famous writers he had known, Hardy was the least likely to say anything which one remembered afterwards. (Sassoon, p. 89)

The homely strength and ripe integrity of his nature was somehow apparent in his avoidance of the brilliant and unusual.
(Sassoon, p. 91)

On the other hand certain 'Keatsian 'characteristics too can be seen; chief of these i the apparent need to go on writing when it was not financially necessary and when he must have known that he had little more to say.

Speaking about ambition T. said today that he had done all that he meant to do, but he did not know whether it had been worth doing.

His only ambition, so far as he could remember, was to have some poem or poems in a good anthology like the Golden Treasury.

The model he had set before him was 'Drink to me only' b Ben Jonson. (*Later Life*, p. 263)

In a letter to Sydney Cockerell, Mrs Hardy makes an

D

interesting comment on Hardy's mood during composition: 'He is now—this afternoon—writing a poem with great spirit; always a sign of well being with him.' Although other interpretations are possible, this looks like a picture of the 'Keatsian' writer at work, and there are a number of poems which strike one as being a form of therapeutic self-expression. There is a striking absence in Hardy's notes and letters of reference to the pains or difficulties of composition and some indication of the reverse: '*Writing* verse gives me great pleasure, but not publishing it' (letter to Cockerell 28 Feb. 1922).

He could also write poems at short notice, on subjects either set for him or provoked by immediate events (e.g. 'The Convergence of the Twain'), just as Keats did, and some of these are good poems. There is, however, an important difference; with Keats the poem is created at the time of writing, and Sutherland points out that it might have ended in a poem very different from the one which actually appeared. With Hardy, total creation is not achieved at the time of composition—the result is strongly conditioned by his previous conclusions and experiences. 'The Convergence of the Twain', for instance, though immediately inspired by the loss of the *Titanic*, is based upon two perennial Hardy themes, the dichotomies of Chance—Predestination and Then-Now.[1]

Edmund Blunden (pp. 262–3) states that the poem on *The Cornhill*, 'The Jubilee of a Magazine', depends on a detail of the cover which is usually unnoticed, but the

---

[1] There is also the possibility of a literary model. One of Hardy's favourite prose passages was Carlyle's description of the slow, silent, unperceived growth of the Oak to its destined end in *The French Revolution* (Part 2, Ch. 1). See *The Fortnightly Review*, xlii (NS), 304–5 (August 1887).

Cornhill cover is merely the starting point for the poem which illustrates another common Hardy theme, the extreme slowness of moral progress (e.g. 'A Christmas Ghost Story' and 'Christmas 1924'). 'V.R. 1819–1901', obviously an 'occasional' piece, repeats the idea expressed in 'A Commonplace Day'. R. P. Blackmur based his harshest criticism of Hardy on the tendency of his patterns of thought to become the subjects of poems.

This characteristic is often disguised because his views were not consciously co-ordinated and were quite capable of being reversed (compare 'Her Immortality' with 'Friends Beyond'). The conclusion differs, but only the conclusion, the theme and tone being almost unchanged. It is hardly surprising, therefore, that most readers have felt the differences were not significant; that in the words of the Tibetan monk, 'The words were not in agreement but the sense was one'.

For about twenty-five years Hardy was chiefly occupied in writing novels; apart from this period, he seems to have maintained a steady output of verse throughout his long life and, although one cannot imagine Hardy in a poetic fever of the 'Keatsian' type, it seems certain that composition of some kind was a necessity. Unfortunately his poetic inspiration tended to the 'Wordsworth' type, depending on recollected emotion, and this was not always available.

When it was lacking, he usually fell back on one or more substitutes which *were* permanently available; re-hashes of previous inspirations, peculiar and macabre incidents, versified 'philosophy' and technical exercises. All these could, and did, produce good poems. They also produced many of the bad and mediocre ones. This process ran all the smoother for the interconnection of certain habits. His 'philosophy', which employed such concepts as Chance, Necessity and Foreknowledge, made him sensitive to their real or apparent operation in the world around him; on the other hand, his typical countryman's store of strange and quirky incidents seemed to illustrate the philosophy; so 'Philosophy' and 'Life' chased each other's tails in the intervals between inspirations.

It was pointed out in Chapter 2 that his spiritual experiences had forced his mind to run in narrow and circular paths, and thus the typical inferior Hardy poem is not the product of a new inspiration, but of an imposed framework derived from previous experiences and inspirations.

This knowledge helps us to understand why the inferior work came into existence; it cannot be used as an excuse for it, but the attempt to separate the poems into those which are to be read and those which are not is not a valuable one. There is a broad intermediate zone in which a little understanding and sympathy make a great deal of difference, and it is this zone which so many people seem to mis-judge or ignore.

More important, perhaps, is the possibility that the good and bad are intimately connected. Frequently the relationship is similar to that between the reverse and obverse sides of a coin; they look very different, but are made from the same metal. For instance, Hardy had an eye for small details almost to the point of obsession: '. . . . he caught sight of a broadsheet, announcing "Family murdered with a penknife". He could not get over that penknife, and kept repeating the word.'[1]

This kind of interest is the source of a poem such as 'The Gap in the White', which tells how a girl cracked a front

[1] Henry W. Nevinson, *Thomas Hardy* (London, 1941), p. 14.

tooth in her sleep and, as a result, lost a very advantageous marriage prospect.

> And if you could go and examine her grave
>> You'd find the gap there,
> But not understand, now that science can save,
>> Her unbounded despair.
>>>> (*Collected Poems*, p. 877)

Here an interest in trivia has produced a trivial poem. 'The Workbox', however, is a very different matter. A girl is having a workbox made from the end of a piece of wood which has been used to make a coffin. She shows distress at the mention of the dead man's name and, though she parries the joiner's inquiries, apologies and explanations, there is obviously more to be told:

> 'Don't, dear, despise my intellect,
>> Mere accidental things
> Of that sort never have effect
>> On my imaginings.'
>
> Yet still her lips were limp and wan,
>> Her face still held aside,
> As if she had known not only John,
>> But known of what he died.
>>>> (*Collected Poems*, p. 374)

This poem is richer in every way and the reasons for this could no doubt be brought out easily enough, but it is clearly based, just as 'The Gap in the White' was, on Hardy's weakness for outré incident and would not have existed without it.

The state of affairs revealed here has been very well described by Clough, talking about Wordsworth:

Had Wordsworth been more capable of discerning his bad from his good, there would, it is likely enough, have been far less of the bad; but the good perhaps would have been very far less good.[1]

F. W. Bateson, who quotes this passage, goes on to remark that 'there ought to be an inherent logical incompatibility between the poetically sublime and the poetically ridiculous, but in Wordsworth's case curiously enough there isn't'.[2] Nor is there in Hardy; he can move spasmodically from one to the other, not only from poem to poem, but within the same poem.

That the good poems have their roots in the same soil as the bad is clear enough, and it is almost equally clear that that soil is frequently one of Hardy's idiosyncrasies. Thus his verbal peculiarities are condemned, but only someone keenly interested in words could have perpetrated some of his gaffes; he is attacked for a fascination with Death, which produced 'The Five Students'; with inability to resolve a philosophic dichotomy, which would relegate 'Nature's Questioning' to a low place; with obsessions about Chance and Predestination ('The Convergence of the Twain' and 'The Wind's Prophecy' are thereby condemned); with crude home-made mythologies ('Hap'); with fixation on the past ('The Self-Unseeing'); with a weakness for slow turgid pondering ('To an Unborn Pauper Child' and 'A Common-place Day').

To wish the weaker poems away is to fall into a version of the fallacy discussed by Edmund Wilson in *The Wound and the Bow*, the fallacy that the advantages of the magic bow of Philoctetes can be obtained without enduring the presence of the loathsome Philoctetes himself.

[1] A. H. Clough, *Poems and Prose Remains* (London, 1869), i, 318–19.
[2] F. W. Bateson, *Wordsworth, A Reinterpretation* (London, 1954), p. 4.

IV

From Idea to Poem

THAT Hardy was not a systematic thinker has been noted by too many people, including Hardy himself, to need emphasising. What does not seem to have been sufficiently appreciated is the extent of the effect this had on his poetry. If he had thought out his philosophy to a conclusion, it is probable that a large proportion of his shorter poems would have remained unwritten. *The Dynasts*, or rather its philosophical 'machinery', embodied his basic assumptions and logically there was no need for any other verse, or at any rate no other philosophical verse.

Hardy's lack of system, however, allowed him from time to time to build on different and sometimes contradictory assumptions. In addition, many of the obsessional patterns, nourished by these assumptions, show the same variety and inconsistency. Chesterton puts it in his usual epigrammatic way:

> . . . the fine literature and very confused cosmic philosophy of Thomas Hardy who tried to say (at the same time) that God did not exist, and that He ought to be ashamed of existing; or possibly that He ought to be ashamed of not existing.[1]

Hardy's enquiries and self-tormentings about the ruling power of the universe continued throughout his life, but seem to have been particularly intense at the end of the

---

[1] G. K. Chesterton, *The Common Man* (London, 1950), p. 198.

1890s, the years preceding *Poems of the Past and the Present*, and *The Dynasts*. About this time William Archer had an interview with Hardy, which was published in *Real Conversations*.

[Hardy]   '... Do you know Hartmann's philosophy of the Unconscious? It suggested to me what seems almost a workable theory of the great problem of the origin of evil—though this, of course, is not Hartmann's own theory—namely, that there may be a consciousness, infinitely far off, at the other end of the chain of phenomena, always striving to express itself, and always baffled and blundering just as the spirits seem to be.'

W. A.   'Is not that simply the good old Manichaean heresy with matter playing the part of the evil principle—Satan, Ahriman, whatever you choose to call it?'

Mr Hardy   'John Stuart Mill somewhere expresses surprise that Manichaeism was not more widely accepted. But is not all popular religion in essence Manichaean? Does it not always postulate a struggle between a principle of good and an independent, if not equally powerful, principle of evil?'[1]

Hardy's 'solution', which he says he developed from von Hartmann, seems to be close to Manichaeism, as Archer says. It is even closer to the Gnostic heresies which were closely associated with Manichaeism.

They [the Gnostics] removed from that supreme Godhead of theirs any tendency to creation, especially any tendency to the creation of matter, and most especially any tendency to the creation of anything capable of 'evil'. They regarded creation in a Deity not so much as impossible as indecent. But they allowed to

---

[1] William Archer, op. cit. pp. 45–6.

It certain emanations or supernatural outputtings and to those yet others, and to those yet others again, until they had imagined 'a long chain of divine creatures, each weaker than its parent', and came at last 'to one, who while powerful enough to create is silly enough not to see that creation is wrong'. This was the God of this world.[1]

Thus, in Hardy, Nature is sometimes represented as making a mistake ('The Mother Mourns'), as continually making mistakes ('The Lacking Sense'), as being unconscious ('The Sleepworker'), or as being completely cut off from God ('God-Forgotten'). There are further variants in 'The Subalterns', 'Doom and She', and numerous other poems.

These poems are best considered as a series of ponderings on the nature of the Universe, Man's relation to it, and the problem of Evil—though some of them are cast in narrative or dialogue form. There is no logical consistency between them; both the premises and the conclusions vary from poem to poem—the only firm ground seems to be that human consciousness is probably an accident and certainly unfortunate; that there is a moral discontinuity between Man and Nature.

Despite this inconsistency (and their lugubrious tone) it is best to read these poems together (many of them are found in the Miscellaneous Poems section of *Poems of the Past and the Present*). Read in this way they re-inforce and interpret each other. Hynes says of 'The Sleepworker' that 'the relation of the Mother to the force which holds her in trance, a very basic question, one would think, is entirely ignored' (p. 39). This is true, but it is unlikely that a persistent reader of Hardy will be troubled by it. Few of these

[1] Charles Williams, *The Descent of the Dove* (2nd ed. London, 1950), p. 23. Inset quotation is from *The Origins of Christianity* by Charles Bigg.

poems are really successful, though the rhetoric of 'The Mother Mourns' is impressive:

> 'Let me grow, then, but mildews and mandrakes,
>   And slimy distortions,
> Let nevermore things good and lovely
>   To me appertain.
>
> 'For Reason is rank in my temples,
>   And Vision unruly,
> And chivalrous laud of my cunning
>   Is heard not again!'

(*Collected Poems*, p. 103)

2

Whatever Hardy may have told Archer, or believed himself, it is unlikely that he needed to read von Hartmann to arrive at these views and, in fact, he gives two likelier sources in this very conversation; 'popular "theology" ' and 'Mill'. He certainly knew something of both.

October 30th (1870) Mother's notion (and also mine) that a figure stands in our van with arm uplifted, to knock us back from any pleasant prospect we indulge in as probable. (*Notebooks*, p. 32)

This note is interesting for several reasons. It illustrates Hardy's remark that popular religion is Manichaean in essence and it is probably an effective source of many of the mis-matings, un-read letters, accidents and unfortunate coincidences which fill his poems and novels. All varieties of Gnosticism posit that the powers ruling the Earth are unpleasant. In some, such as Manichaeism, they are *absolutely* evil, running the world just as they please to the torment of the human race—who are knocked back from any pleasant prospect which they indulge in as probable. Hardy obviously could have absorbed this from his mother while very young, long before he had a chance to work out a philosophy for himself.

The commoner view, however, is that the World Powers are merely ignorant, incompetent and bungling; subalterns in fact, though rebelling against, or ignorant of, the true commander. This distinction, brought to the everyday level, results in the uncertainty familiar to all readers of Hardy, as to whether disasters are the result of malevolence or accident. Here we have another example of Hardy being blamed for an intellectual weakness which is shared by people of much higher philosophical standing.

The influence of Mill on Hardy has often been under-estimated, probably because by the time he was important enough to attract interviewers he had read Schopenhauer and von Hartmann and tended to refer to them rather than to his earlier favourites. Thus, on 5 February 1898, he made a memorandum suggesting a poem on the theme of a non-omnipotent God. It is accompanied by a reference (inserted by Hardy or his second wife) to McTaggart's *Some Dogmas of Religion* (*Later Years*, pp. 73–4). But this theory is discussed in Mill's *Three Essays on Religion* (1874), which Hardy must have read, since it is the source of Mill's remarks about Manichaeism. Mill points out that it and similar creeds are the only 'form of belief in the super-natural' which 'stands wholly clear both of intellectual contradiction and of moral obliquity' (p. 116), and states that 'popular Christianity' is merely inconsistent Dualism.

The only difference on this matter between popular Christianity and the religion of Ormuzd and Ahriman is that the former pays its good Creater the bad compliment of having been the maker of the Devil and of being at all times able to crush him and his evil deeds and counsels, which nevertheless he does not do. (pp. 183-4)

As we have seen, Hardy believed that sentience had been born by accident into a world never intended to contain it. Mill deals with the point too.

That nothing can consciously produce Mind but Mind is self evident, being involved in the meaning of the words; but that there cannot be unconscious production must not be assumed, for it is the very point to be proved. (p. 152)

Alfred Noyes said that he had 'never been able to conceive a Cause of Things that could be less in any respect than the things caused' (*Later Years*, p. 218), and others have echoed this objection, but if someone of the ratiocinative power of Mill could regard the question as open, then Hardy can hardly be blamed for doing the same.[1]

Finally, Hardy's 'evolutionary meliorism' discussed in the Preface to *Late Lyrics* and elsewhere has seemed to some readers at odds with the rest of his philosophy.

That the Unconscious Will of the Universe is growing aware of Itself I believe I may claim as my own idea solely—at which I arrived by reflecting that what has already taken place in a fraction of the whole (i.e. so much of the world as has become conscious) is likely to take place in the mass; and there being no

[1] To the best of my knowledge none of the searchers for the origin of *The Dynasts* has considered page 133 of Mill's *Three Essays*: 'Setting out therefore from the scientific view of Nature as a connected system, or united whole, united not like a web composed of separate threads in passive juxtaposition with one another but rather like the human or animal frame, an apparatus kept going by perpetual action and reaction among all its parts. . . .' The collocation of web, human frame, action and reaction seems significant.

will outside the mass—that is, the Universe—the whole Will becomes conscious thereby: and ultimately, it is to be hoped, sympathetic. (*Later Years*, pp. 124-5)

But given the premises, the existence and basic nature of the unconscious will, this seems logical enough and is certainly meliorism, though of a rather pale kind. This was probably, despite frequent moments of despair, Hardy's belief during the last twenty years of his life. It is, at bottom, an optimistic and activist creed since as a philosophical position it is similar to that of the Non-Omnipotent Power of Good which, as Mill points out, might be able to get its way only very slowly and need 'even the smallest help to the right side' from 'the humblest human creature' (Mill, p. 256). He makes a similar point in an eloquent passage in *Utilitarianism*.

All the grand sources, in short, of human suffering are in a great degree, many of them almost entirely, conquerable by human care and effort; and though their removal is grievously slow—though a long succession of generations will perish in the breach before the conquest is completed, and this world becomes all that, if will and knowledge were not wanting, it might easily be made—yet every mind sufficiently intelligent and generous to bear a part, however small and unconspicuous, in the endeavour, will draw a noble enjoyment from the conquest itself, which he would not for any bribe in the form of selfish indulgence consent to be without.

Reasonably enough, Hardy asked in 'He Wonders about Himself' if his mind was 'sufficiently intelligent and gener-ous' to play his small part in the conquest.

> Part is mine of the general Will,
> Cannot my share in the sum of sources

Bend a digit the poise of forces,
And a fair desire fulfil?

(*Collected Poems*, pp. 479–80)

Meliorism also helps to ease a major contradiction in Hardy's thought. The conception of the mechanical, indifferent, universe is, of course, logically incompatible with the 'Manichaean' conception of the hostile one. The same entity cannot be both immoral and amoral, conscious and unconscious, hostile and indifferent. Philosophically it seems impossible to resolve this contradiction, but from a purely 'human' point of view the difference shrinks considerably since humanity, on either theory, is engaged in a long, hard, painful, but *not necessarily* losing battle.

I think that enough has already been said to show that Hardy had plenty of opportunity to absorb various philosophic ideas, but in view of the close connection that he seems to have had with Leslie Stephen, it may be worth noting that when the latter's father, Sir James Stephen, was appointed Regius Professor of Modern History at Cambridge, 'Dr. Corrie, the Master of Jesus College, wagged his head at Archdeacon Hardwick, "Who would have thought we should have seen a live Gnostic walking about the streets of Cambridge?" '[1]

3

We have seen that Hardy had philosophical ideas, obsessions or intuitions which he was unable either to settle or to leave alone. This may have played a big part in making him a poet; it certainly made him the kind of poet he was. G. K. Chesterton said of Tennyson that he had no special

---

[1] N. G. Annan, *Leslie Stephen* (London, 1951), p. 43.

talent for being a philosophic poet but he had a special *vocation* for being a philosophic poet; the remark seems even more fruitful when applied to Hardy, because his philosophic ideas created poems which do not discuss them directly far more often than did Tennyson's. Thus Hardy's doubt as to the existence, identity and power of the Ruler of the Universe, sometimes aired directly, is frequently discussed in terms of some secondary, derivative, problem or partly concealed by being placed in some particular situation. One of these derivative problems is that of Chance v. Design, which often appears in a local context as the Meeting or Not Meeting of two people, frequently actual or potential lovers.

The connection here is fairly obvious. When the idea of a Guiding Providence is rejected, the problem of whether events are predetermined or casual becomes pressing—and difficult. 'But Chance, as an idea, is a chameleon in its behaviour. Place it upon one twig of circumstance, and it will suggest an impact of blind fate; upon another, and it seems a junction of two determinate life-lines'.[1] *Wessex Poems*, Hardy's first serious appearance as a poet, has this problem serving as a basis in five out of the first six poems ('Amabel' is the exception). Poems of this kind, like all his work, vary greatly in value, but, generally, they are at their best when they are personal (which usually means springing from the Wordsworthian process considered earlier) or when they embody an incident precise, but not autobiographical. One might, sacrificing accuracy for succinctness, call them 'private' and 'public'. Thus in 'The Convergence of the Twain', the precise vision and the philosophic theory support and fit each other like 'twin halves of one august event'.

[1] McDowall, p. 30.

iii

Over the mirrors meant
To glass the opulent
The seaworm crawls—grotesque, slimed, dumb, indifferent.

viii

And as the smart ship grew
In stature, grace, and hue,
In shadowy silent distance grew the Iceberg too.

xi

Till the Spinner of the Years
Said 'Now!' And each one hears,
And consummation comes, and jars two hemispheres.

(*Collected Poems*, pp. 288–9)

The second half of the poem would, by itself, be a power-
ful application or illustration of the philosophy; only when
allied to the sensuous immediacy of the first half does a
great poem come into being.

One could not say this of 'The Wind's Prophecy', of
which the second stanza is a fair specimen:

A distant verge morosely gray
Appears, while clots of flying foam
Break from its muddy monochrome,
And a light blinks up far away.
I sigh: 'My eyes now as all day
Behold her ebon loops of hair!'
Like bursting bonds the wind responds
'Nay, wait for tresses flashing fair!'

(*Collected Poems*, p. 464)

I think that if Wordsworth could have seen this poem he
might have used it in his Preface instead of the Sonnet by

Gray, as an even clearer example of good and bad poetic language. In all five stanzas, amazingly, the vigour and accuracy of the first half is opposed by the 'literary' slackness of the second; 'clots of flying foam' against 'ebon loops'. Furthermore, this division corresponds with that between 'Experience' and 'Philosophy' since the poem is so obviously autobiographical that its inspiration can be placed exactly: 7 March 1870, on the Launceston-St Juliot Road; the often remembered day of his first visit to Cornwall. (It is only fair to point out that one item of the description *could* be of later origin. In 1875 while living at Swanage, Hardy noted: 'On the left Durlstone Head roaring high and low, like a giant asleep' (*Early Life*, p. 142). Although Hardy sometimes repeated his images, this is probably the origin of the line

> Snores like a giant in his sleep.

If so, it is significant of Hardy's methods of handling his sources of inspiration that this, not part of the original scene, is the only line which was revised; to

> Snores like old Skrymer in his sleep.)

Although formally the second halves are the core of the poem, poetically they are awkward, inferior codas.

'In Vision I Roamed' shows something different again. Here, 'philosophy' is obviously the starting point of the poem; equally obviously Hardy has failed, or never attempted, to give any precise embodiment to it, relying instead on vague cosmic visions; a procedure which brings its own punishment in vapid adjectives like 'ghast' and 'monstrous', the alliteration of the last two lines, the ugly assonance of lines 3 and 13, and capitals used lavishly in an attempt to get the significance which the words themselves

E

have failed to win. And this was after revision; the first edition had, for instance, as line 11

> Who might have been set on some outstep sphere.

In terms of the distinction made above, it is neither private nor public, but merely a whimsy.

Lastly, a stanza from 'Ditty':

> To feel I might have kissed—
> Loved as true—
> Otherwhere, nor Mine have missed
> My life through,
> Had I never wandered near her,
> Is a smart severe—severer
> In the thought that she is nought,
> Even as I, beyond the dells
> Where she dwells.
>
> (*Collected Poems*, p. 14)

This is in a sense personal, since the poem is dedicated to Hardy's first wife (the only poem to be so). But it lacks a precise inspiration, that is, any connection with a definite occurrence, and was written in 1870, soon after Hardy met Emma Gifford; it was, therefore, not a product of the typical lying-fallow period. The result is, not unexpectedly, a competent—even charming—but unimportant piece of verse.

4

With his views on necessitation, or at the most a very limited free will, events seemed to show him a fancy he had often held and expressed, that the never-ending push of the Universe was an unpurposive and irresponsible groping in the direction of the least resistance, might be the real truth. (*Later Years*, pp. 165–6)

Such views, even if held only as a fancy, would tend to give importance to Chance for at least two reasons. It would be both result and symbol of the actual order of things; 'the never ending push of the Universe' might, from the human point of view, be in any direction or series of directions; happiness, disaster, absurdity and coincidence could happen without apparent rhyme or reason. Secondly, even when a human choice could be made and any particular course taken, there was ample opportunity for it to turn out to have been the wrong one.

Thus, in 'The Dame of Athelhall' the eloping wife returns to her husband for his sake, only to find that he is glad of her departure and admires her for her initiative in taking it.

> So Time rights all things in long, long years—
> Or rather she, by her bold design!
> I admire a woman no balk deters:
> > She has blessed my life, in fine.
> > > (*Collected Poems*, p. 143)

In 'The Curate's Kindness', the zealous 'young Pa'son' persuades the Workhouse Guardians to allow a new entrant to be with his wife; in fact their potential segregation had been his sole comfort.

> ... To get freed of her there was the one thing
> Had made the change welcome to me.
> > (*Collected Poems*, p. 195)

These are the results of conscious choice, but 'hunches' and spiritual presentiments fare no better; see, for instance, the almost pathetic irony of 'A Wife Comes Back'.

This kind of incident has made his work notorious, though the attack is usually directed at the prose works where the demand for, and expectation of, realism is greater. (Hardy's remarks about the Inquisition leaving Galileo alone if he had written in verse are applicable to more than embodied ideas.) It is clear, however, that the coincidences, accidents, and so forth are not always the expedients of a careless author, but frequently part of a rational if somewhat ramshackle system of thought.[1] Allied to these incidents are those which show how human happiness and destiny are balanced upon a fine edge and that a trifle may decide much, as in 'At the Word "Farewell" '.

> 'I am leaving you . . . Farewell!' I said
> As I followed her on
> By an alley bare boughs overspread;
> 'I soon must be gone!'
> Even then the scale might have turned
> Against love by a feather,
> —But crimson one cheek of hers burned
> When we came in together.
>
> (*Collected Poems*, p. 406)

This is a successful, if not important, poem; 'He inadvertently Cures his Love-pains (Song)' is not successful. As Blunden points out, 'The word "Song" prefixed to an item is to be considered as a warning that what follows will not be in Hardy's strongest way of sense or fancy' (p. 245), but the main cause of this poem's inferiority is that it is obviously a concocted situation; and Hardy is rarely successful in such cases. Here, although the core of the incident is

[1] 'History is rather a stream than a tree. There is nothing organic in its shape, nothing systematic in its development. It flows on like a thunderstorm-rill by a road-side; now a straw turns it this way, now a tiny barrier of sand that. The offhand decision of some commonplace mind high in office at a critical moment influences the course of events for a hundred years.' (*Early Life*, p. 225)

described in far more detail than in 'At the Word Farewell', the incident and poem seem thin and perfunctory compared with the rich ambience and the pressure of recollection found in the latter. It would be a mistake to assume that these are conscious or deliberate illustrations of the 'philosophy'. Everything points to the fact that Hardy had the villager's interest in these village stories for their own sake; nowhere did he show his peasant ancestry more plainly. The truth is, probably, that the 'philosophy' inhibited critical discrimination among these poems. In any case, we have already seen his defence.

> ... as, in looking at a carpet, by following one colour a certain pattern is suggested, by following another colour, another; so in life the seer should watch that pattern among general things which his idiosyncrasy moves him to observe, and that alone.

> (*Early Life*, p. 198)

This, of course, provides a theoretical justification of practically anything; it needs, however, something more to convince us that 'The Dame of Athelhall', 'In the Days of the Crinoline' and 'A Woman's Fancy' are, in the last resort anything more than oddities.

(It should be remembered nevertheless that Hardy seemed to attract 'Hardyish' situations around himself. Siegfried Sassoon, Sir Newman Flower and Sir John Squire, among others, noticed this; an example is seen in the incident of the dying woman told on page 35 of *Later Years*.)[1]

What ruins many poems of this type is not the matter nor its repetition, distressing though this can be, but the

---

[1] It is also profitable to consult Marcel Chicoteau's *Essay on the 'Ephectic' Attitude in regard to Destiny; Seneca – Racine – Hardy* (Cardiff, 1941). M. Chicoteau does something to put Hardy's coincidences in respectable company and, perhaps, on a decent philosophical footing.

failure of technique or, perhaps, the failure to employ any:
'.... we see it as weakness, as substitution, precisely as
work not done' (Blackmur, p. 53).

Closely allied to the patterns mentioned above is the
'Had I but known' pattern; the poem which recounts the
failure to realise the significance of some moment or action
is an obvious pendent to the poem which describes the
wrong action. The pattern, diffused through many poems,
appears in almost pure form in such poems as 'The Tem-
porary the All', 'Best Times', 'You on the Tower', 'Known
had I' and 'The Musical Box'. Two of these, 'The Musical
Box' and 'You on the Tower', occur within a few pages of,
each other in *Moments of Vision* and thus seem to be fair
material for comparison (one of the intervening poems, 'The
Last Performance' has a modified version of this pattern as
its basis).

The Musical Box

Lifelong to be
Seemed the fair colour of the time:
That there was standing shadowed near
A spirit who sang to the gentle chime
Of the self-struck notes, I did not hear,
I did not see.

Thus did it sing
To the mindless lyre that played indoors
As she came to listen for me without:
'O value what the nonce outpours—
This best of life—that shines about
Your welcoming!'

I had slowed along
After the torrid hours were done,

Though still the posts and walls and road
Flung back their sense of the hot-faced sun,
And had walked by Stourside Mill, where broad
    Stream-lilies throng.

    And I descried
The dusky house that stood apart,
And her, white-muslined, waiting there
In the porch with high-expectant heart,
While still the thin mechanic air
    Went on inside.

    At whiles would flit
Swart bats, whose wings, be-webbed and tanned,
Whirred like the wheels of ancient clocks:
She laughed a hailing as she scanned
Me in the gloom, the tuneful box
    Intoning it.

    Lifelong to be
I thought it. That there watched hard by
A spirit who sang to the indoor tune,
'O make the most of what is nigh!'
I did not hear in my dull soul-swoon—
    I did not see.

        (*Collected Poems*, pp. 453–4)

According to some of the critical dicta which have found
favour in this century,' The Musical Box' should be a very
bad poem; three quarters of it at least seems irrelevant; the
heat, the mill, the lilies, the bats, etc.; there is no necessary
reason why the spirit should sing or indeed be present at all;
the part played by the musical box seems over-emphasized;
and the 'advice' is hardly profound. As the poem is successful
despite all this, it obviously needs closer analysis.

It seems almost certain that the scene was an actual one and the sense of this has got into the poem. The lilies, heat, bats, and so on are not beautiful padding, but pledges of truth and actuality besides being creators of it. The mechanical, monotonous tinkle creates the answering tinkle of the spirit's song by its very regularity. The box's mechanical continuity, emphasized by 'self-struck' and 'mindless', which is obviously an effective cause of the listener's belief that his happiness will last for ever (note that it is intoning a welcome as well as evoking the spirit's song), extends itself deep into his perception of everything else, even the bats which

Whirred like the wheels of ancient clocks.

Thus, when the final 'I did not see' is reached, the triteness of the adage has been scoured away and it seems as if minted anew.

'You on the Tower', on the other hand, which seems to have so much immediate relevance, firm structure, lack of padding, in its favour, is, in fact, far more perfunctory and mechanical than the musical box of the first poem ever was. A reader who knew a fair amount of Hardy would, I think, fear the worst at the end of the first line, 'You on the tower of my factory—'. Hardy's non-rustic dialogue is frequently something to be endured rather than enjoyed and a factory could not be anything to him other than a vague symbol, vague because backed up neither by precise knowledge nor intuitive understanding. (There is one poem by Hardy in Jeremy Warburg's anthology, *The Industrial Muse, the Industrial Revolution in English Poetry*, but the compiler specifically mentions it as an example of the kind of viewpoint which 'provides little more than an "occasion" for a poem'.) There is nothing to distract attention from the triteness of the theme and structure; certainly not the language, whose mixture of slang and 'poetese' is left cruelly exposed.

Hardy could frequently invest his own experiences with poetic significance; sometimes he found that his intuitions could crystallise upon an objective event; only rarely could he invent a successful 'myth', and I think that this is at the bottom of the difference in merit of these two poems.

The search for certainty about the existence and nature of the Prime Mover frequently leads to attempts to obtain knowledge from that presumed Prime Mover's most obvious handiwork, Nature. The poems on the subject however, are usually genuinely agnostic; they celebrate not the gaining of knowledge, but the realization of the impossibility of getting it; for instance 'The Blinded Bird', 'The Darkling Thrush', 'An August Midnight', 'The Caged Thrush Freed and home again', 'A Backward Spring' and 'The Year's Awakening' with its repeated awe-struck enquiry—'How do you know?' This type of poem seems to be the chief exception to the remarks above about Hardy's successful poems. However, they are about matters within his frequent observation and even here one sometimes suspects some precise inspiration, e.g. 'The Darkling Thrush' and 'An August Midnight'.

5

Hardy's speculations about 'the President of the Immortals' can hardly be separated from what Blackmur calls his 'triple obsession with death, memory and time'.[1] His

[1] Blackmur, p. 60. The phrase may have been inspired by Hardy's 'To Life'. 'I know what thou wouldst tell/ Of Death, Time, Destiny.'

interest in the first of these has helped to bring him into critical disrepute; for example, Hynes on 'Lodging-House Fuchsias': 'All in all, the poem asks of us a greater emotional response to the mere *fact* of mortality than we are likely to give' (p. 52).

This opinion is, of course, incontrovertible on the personal level and it may be defensible as a critical judgement on the poem, but I suspect that the attitude revealed here is likely be an inhibiting one generally. No doubt there have always been those who, like Mrs Peachum, 'never meddle in matters of Death', or who, like Saki's Reginald, have suffered from untimely pathos: '. . . . favoured us with a long recitation about a little girl who died or did something equally hackneyed . . .'; but the contemporary indifference or numbness seems to be unusual, if not unprecedented. Mr E. M. Forster is near enough to Hardy's generation for his remarks to have special value.

Death, though it interests me personally, for I am bound to experience it, is at present an unfashionable subject. It is regarded as insufficiently communal. Thanks to two world wars and the possibility of a third, the present century has become very offhand and gruff on the topic of death. Get on with your job! If you fall out of it someone else will carry on. I realized what was coming a few years ago, when I referred in a broadcast to a poem of Matthew Arnold's ('A Southern Night') in which he laments emotionally, and I thought appropriately, on the deaths of his brother and his brother's wife. I received as a result a rather dry letter from a member of the Arnold family, who took my sentimentality to task. . . . Anyhow my correspondent was in closer touch than I can be with contemporary taste. He had duly relegated death to the statistical.[1]

[1] 'De Senectute' in *London Magazine*, Nov. 1957.

Anyone who has noticed the prominence of the 'Hiro-shima-Auschwitz' poem in contemporary poetry can have little doubt that Forster's correspondent is indeed typical; death has apparently to be 'global', sudden or specially appalling to make much impression.[1] And yet, as Chesterton says somewhere, Death is more tragic than death by drowning. If Hardy seems to spend too much time in the graveyard and sometimes to be a little too much at his ease there, it is well to remember that he has many literary ancestors who shared this taste, and that this is one of the habits in which his rural upbringing and closeness to the emotions of the common man show clearly. We might compare the notorious last two lines of Tennyson's 'Enoch Arden'. No doubt it would have been better for Tennyson's reputation if he had never written these lines, but he showed that he was closer to the feelings of his fisher folks than his critics are.

What we find in fact is that Hardy wrote both well and badly on this subject, as on most others. About one-third of his poems refer to Death in some way and about a fifteenth are set in graveyards. These proportions, though high, are less than is commonly thought, just as the number of 'philosophic' poems is. What usually surprises anyone who examines the whole body of the poems is the large proportion of love poems; for example, Hardy himself when faced with a classification of his poems, 'I see there are most poems on "Love and Marriage". More than on "Death"—which I am told I am always bringing in....'[2]

The preponderance of these two categories would not

[1] Edward Lucie-Smith has noted the frequency of this theme in modern verse. ('The Tortured Yearned as Well' in *Critical Quarterly*, iv (1962), p. 38.)
[2] Vere H. Collins, *Talks with Thomas Hardy at Max Gate, 1920–22* (1928), p. 20.

have surprised Yeats. 'From all which you will see that I am still of opinion that only two topics can be of the least interest to a serious and studious mind—sex and the dead.'[1] Some of the implications of this opinion will be considered later. For the moment all that need be said is that it supports the view that Hardy's persistent interest in the subject of Death is merely a heightening of the normal human interest; most of the apparent exaggeration or perversity is due to the movement of present-day interest in the opposite direction. In short, as with the 'philosophy', a little historical knowledge, insight and sympathy will put the reader in a receptive frame of mind—and the reader who is not will get little from him, since he has not the manifest attractions which compel readers almost against their will. Then it becomes obvious that he uses Death and burial as a kind of touchstone or datum point from which a life, character or action can be surveyed or assessed. The value of the poem is not necessarily changed by this realization; but the reasonableness of the method is shown, which is helpful, since prejudice against this kind of subject can hinder enjoyment of some very fine poems.

Few are likely to think of 'Her Late Husband' as anything other than an oddity, but one can see clearly how the act of burial becomes symbolic and the peg for social criticism:

> 'O strange interment! Civilised lands
>   Afford few types thereof;
> Here is a man who takes his rest
>   Beside his very Love,
> Beside the one who was his wife
>   In our sight up above!'

(Collected Poems, p. 152)

[1] The Letters of W. B. Yeats (London, 1954), ed. Alan Wade, p. 730.

'Julie-Jane' is harder to assess; for one thing, the typical Hardyan mixture of dialect, accuracy, 'literaryness', recollected emotion and syntactical awkwardness can be seen within the same stanza:

> Laugh; how 'a would laugh!
> Her peony lips would part
> As if none such a place for a lover to quaff
> At the deeps of a heart.
>
> (*Collected Poems*, p. 229)

and there is what seems to be also a typical inability to keep a King Charles's Head out of the poem:

> —Yes,
> That's her burial bell.

On the other hand, the 'burial' core of the poem helps to bring the lively insouciance of the girl into sharper focus:

> Bubbling and brightsome eyed!
> But now—O never again:
> She chose her bearers before she died
> From her fancy men.

Again, 'Her Dilemma' may be of inferior value, but without its setting would be of none whatever:

> The two were silent in a sunless church,
> Whose mildewed walls, uneven paving-stones,
> And wasted carvings passed antique research;
> And nothing broke the clock's dull monotones.
>
> (*Collected Poems*, p. 10)

These are the average products of the soil in which his imagination was nourished; the best fruits are something which few could wish away or to be any other than they are; for example 'Friends Beyond':

'Gone', I call them, gone for good, that group of local hearts and
                                        heads;
            Yet at mothy curfew-tide,
And at midnight when the noon-heat breathes it back from walls
                                        and leads,

(*Collected Poems*, p. 52)

or 'Voices from Things Growing in a Churchyard':

            These flowers are I, poor Fanny Hurd,
                    Sir or Madam,
            A little girl here sepultured.
            Once I flit-fluttered like a bird
            Above the grass, as now I wave
            In daisy shapes above my grave,
                    All day cheerily,
                    All night eerily.

(*Collected Poems*, p. 590)

or 'The Dead Quire':

            The singers had followed one by one,
            Treble, and tenor, and thorough-base;
            And the worm that wasteth had begun
                    To mine their mouldering place.

(*Collected Poems*, p. 240)

To say that the problem of Death is virtually the same as
that of Immortality is only too obvious, but it may not be
quite so obvious that, to many minds, it is virtually the same
as that of the existence of God.

This problem of the existence of God, a problem that is
rationally insoluble, is really identical with the problem of
consciousness . . . it is none other than the problem of the sub-
stantial existence of the soul, the problem of the perpetuity of the
human soul, the problem of the human finality of the universe

itself. To believe in a living and personal God, in an eternal and universal consciousness that knows and loves us, is to believe that the Universe exists *for* man.[1]

As with the 'philosophic' views, the poems consider the problem directly and indirectly with varying degrees of success, and with varying, sometimes contradictory, conclusions. Thus, in contradiction to 'Friends Beyond' we have the theme of Immortality as Being Remembered with its corollary that Death is essentially Being Forgotten.[2] When the theme is tackled directly by Hardy, which is comparatively rare, the usual weaknesses appear, since normally he has difficulty when he can neither draw upon his own resources of memory nor find a satisfactory objective embodiment of the theme. Thus, we have the factitiousness of 'Her Immortality', though, like many of his failures,

[1] Miguel de Unamuno, *The Tragic Sense of Life* (London, 1921), p. 182. Cited as Unamuno.

[2] This seems to have been a feature of nineteenth-century agnostic thought. It is discussed, for instance, in A. E. Crawley's *Idea of the Soul* (London, 1909), is mentioned, to be rejected, by Unamuno (p. 16); and is found in Samuel Butler (*Erewhon Revisited* and the sonnet 'Not on Stygian Shore'). An early literary handling is found in a sonnet by Thomas Hood:

> It is not death that sometime in a sigh
> This eloquent breath shall take its speechless flight;
> That sometime these bright stars, that now reply
> In sunlight to the sun, shall set in night;
> That this warm conscious flesh shall perish quite,
> And all life's ruddy springs forget to flow;
> That thoughts shall cease, and the immortal spright
> Be lapp'd in alien clay and laid below;
> It is not death to know this;—but to know
> That pious thoughts, which visit at new graves
> In tender pilgrimage, will cease to go
> So duly and so oft,—and when grass waves
> Over the past-away, there may be then
> No resurrection in the minds of Men.

this poem can grow on one. 'His Immortality', on the other hand, has a clear, obvious, line and a fine gloom of its own.

Hardy's triumph with this theme, however, is 'Friends Beyond', where he has succeeded in placing his idea in a clearly realized situation, with characters whose ambitions and daily life were part of his experience; instead of a name-less bare space we have Stinsford Churchyard (this is made quite clear by the illustration in the first edition); instead of unknown cardboard figures, people like William Dewy and Lady Susan, whose lives and characters had nourished his imagination.

Readers of Yeats are familiar with the fact that implausible beliefs can provide an excellent mental framework for poetry, and poems by Hardy also show this. (Both poets, to some extent, regarded these beliefs as poetically useful myths, and were not always prepared to assert them outside the poem.) Several show immortality achieved by a sort of vegetable metamorphosis or transmigration, e.g. 'Voices from Things Growing in a Churchyard', 'Shelley's Skylark' and 'Transformations'. All of them are fine poems, though the last is rather embarrassingly explicit,

> Portion of this yew
> Is a man my grandsire knew,
> Bosomed here at its foot:
> This branch may be his wife,
> A ruddy human life
> Now turned to a green shoot.

> (*Collected Poems*, p. 443)

The original inspiration for this could easily have come from Fitzgerald's 'Rubaiyat', but Hardy's profession as church restorer and his predilection for graveyards could keep the whimsy in mind, or even suggest it to him. Why it should interest him as a speculation is obvious enough.

One way in which a man can be regarded as surviving is in the person of his descendants, and theories of Immortality have been built upon the perpetuation of the individual in his children, family or even race. 'Heredity', with its especially significant second and final lines, has the succinct finality of an epigram and yet arouses reverberations that extend far beyond its ostensible subject:

> I am the family face;
> Flesh perishes, I live on,
> Projecting trait and trace
> Through time to times anon,
> And leaping from place to place
> Over oblivion.
>
> The years-heired feature that can
> In curve and voice and eye
> Despise the human span
> Of durance—that is I;
> The eternal thing in man,
> That heeds no call to die.
>
> > (*Collected Poems*, pp. 407–8)

If perpetuation in descendants is a kind of immortality, then childlessness or extinction of a family line is a kind of death, and this is handled in 'She, I and They', where the two are almost certainly Hardy and one of his sisters:

> Half in dreaming
> 'Then its meaning,'
> Said we, 'must be surely this; that they repine

F

That we should be the last
Of stocks once unsurpassed,
And unable to keep up their sturdy line.

(*Collected Poems*, pp. 408-9)

There is a little evidence that their childlessness was one of the reasons for the domestic unhappiness of Hardy and his first wife, and his will reveals the sad fact that at the age of eighty-two he still hoped to have a son! (Evelyn Hardy, p. 322). Such poems as 'To a Motherless Child' and 'Her Death and After' become more interesting and significant when viewed in the light of this.

The number of love poems is always a surprise to readers not well acquainted with Hardy's work; this is not a contradiction of his obsessions about Death and Immortality, but part of them. Yeats's comment shows a connection between Love and Death and Unamuno makes it explicit:

The vanity of the passing world and love are the two fundamental and heart-penetrating notes of true poetry. And they are two notes of which neither can be sounded without causing the other to vibrate. The feeling of the vanity of the passing world kindles love in us, the only thing that triumphs over the vain and transitory, the only thing that fills life again and eternalizes it.

(Unamuno, p. 39)

Later he remarks that 'in love and by love we seek to perpetuate ourselves' (p. 133).

6

Hardy, who was an amateur philosopher ('I read *Mind* occasionally'), counted Einstein among the philosophers and showed some interest in the theory of Relativity, of which he gives his own interpretation in that remarkable poem, 'Drinking Song':

> And now comes Einstein with a notion—
> > Not quite yet clear
> > To many here—
> That there's no time, no space, no motion,
> > Nor rathe nor late,
> > Nor square nor straight,
> But just a sort of bending-ocean.
>
> > *(Collected Poems*, p. 866)

What interested him here, of course, is the possibility of permanent existence and a notebook entry makes this quite clear:

> Relativity. That things and events always were, are and will be (e.g. E. M. F. etc. are living still in the past). *(Notebooks*, p. 99)[1]

He used this as the basis for at least three poems, 'The Absolute Explains', 'So, Time', and 'In a Museum'. An inkling of the variety with which Hardy can deal with the same idea, despite the popular impression to the contrary, may be got by comparing the extract from 'Drinking Song' with this from 'The Absolute Explains', with its turgid, awkward, yet impressive, pondering.

> Know, Time is toothless, seen all through;
> > The Present, that men but see,
> Is phasmal: since in a sane purview
> > All things are shaped to be
> > Eternally.
>
> > *(Collected Poems*, p. 716)

---

[1] The three initials probably stand for Emma, Mary and Florence, Hardy's first wife, sister and second wife, though the last was still alive.

The third poem, 'In a Museum', is different again, a smoothly flowing lyric:

> Here's the mould of a musical bird long passed from light,
> Which over the earth before man came was winging;
>
> *(Collected Poems*, p. 404)

This desire to abolish, ignore or, at least, halt time is the main motivation of a number of poems, the ostensible subject-matter and structures of which vary considerably. The common factor seems to be a wish to arrest the flux of Time and Change, or to limit their action, or in some way to stand outside them, and thus, in a sense, to approach Immortality. It is accompanied by a keen, almost diseased, sensitivity to the effect of Time and Change on Man, his Works, Nature, and the Earth itself.

> It is the on-going—i.e. the 'becoming'—of the world that produces its sadness. If the world stood still at a felicitous moment there would be no sadness in it.   *(Early Life*, p. 265)

Explicit statements of this theme are rare, but we find one in 'Childhood among the Ferns,' where, after a delicate piece of description, comes

> I said: 'I could live on here thus till death';
>
> And queried in the green rays as I sate:
> 'Why should I have to grow to man's estate,
> And this afar-noised World perambulate?'
>
> *(Collected Poems*, p. 825)

This is based on an incident in Hardy's own childhood, perhaps before any of these problems began to worry him, but the interesting thing is that the memory and significance of the incident seem to have lasted throughout his life.

It is used in *Jude the Obscure* (page 15), while 'Childhood among the Ferns' appeared in Hardy's last collection and could have written when he was eighty-seven.

An obvious pendant to Hardy's sensitivity to the passage and effects of Time is his awareness of, and wish to grasp the Moment. If the Moment, somehow, contains All, then the passage of Time is less important, perhaps a kind of illusion. Seconds matter very much; aeons very little ('The moment one and infinite' of Browning's 'By the Fireside', Wordsworth's 'spots of time', Joyce's 'epiphany' come to mind, besides Hardy's own 'Moments of Vision'). As often, it is hard to illustrate the use of a theme because of a tendency to combine with others, in this case that of Ignorance of What is to Come; (for instance 'Under High Stoy Hill'). Different aspects can be seen, however, in 'Moments of Vision', 'On the Departure Platform' and most explicitly in 'The History of an Hour' with its clinching final line, 'So catch that hour'.

One way in which this dream of Arresting the Flux shows itself is in his conviction that there is a basic permanence in simple things. The best known example is in 'In Time of the "Breaking of Nations"'.

> Yonder a maid and her wight
> Come whispering by:
> War's annals will cloud into night
> Ere their story die.

(Collected Poems, p. 511)

It is found in the badly flawed, yet striking, 'Souls of the Slain' and in 'Life and Death at Sunrise'. The latter combines effectively a number of the themes connected with Arresting of the Flux and Immortality.

Life and Death at Sunrise
(Near Dogbury Gate, 1867)

The hills uncap their tops
Of woodland, pasture, copse,
And look on the layers of mist
At their foot that still persist:
They are like awakened sleepers on one elbow lifted,
Who gaze around to learn if things during night have shifted.

A wagon creaks up from the fog
With a laboured leisurely jog;
Then a horseman from off the hill-tip
Comes clapping down into the dip;
While woodlarks, finches, sparrows, try to entune at one time,
And cocks and hens and cows and bulls take up the chime.

With a shouldered basket and flagon
A man meets the one with the wagon,
And both the men halt of long use.
'Well', the waggoner says, 'What's the news?'
'—'Tis a boy this time. You've just met the doctor trotting back.
She's doing very well. And we think we shall call him "Jack".'

'And what have you got covered there?'
He nods to the waggon and mare.
'Oh, a coffin for old John Thinn:
We are just going to put him in.'
'—So he's gone at last. He always had a good constitution.'
'—He was ninety-odd. He could call up the French Revolution.'

(*Collected Poems*, pp. 692–3)

This poem appears to be a product of the lying fallow period which produced much of Hardy's better verse. (We have no record of the date of writing the poem, but it appeared in 1925 in *Human Shows* and the MS, according to

Purdy has the title ‚'A long-ago Sunrise at Dogbury Gate'.)[1]
And indeed the poem is placed firmly in a setting of steady
rural living and labouring that seems likely to continue
'though Dynasties pass'; the wagon 'creaks' and moves
'with a laboured leisurely jog', the father has 'a shouldered
basket and flagon', and 'both the men halt of long use'.
This particular day is slightly unusual (symbolized by the
doctor who hastily and noisily 'comes clapping down into
the dip'), but the birth and death are laconically expected
and accepted as part of the rhythm of life: ' 'Tis a boy this
time'; 'so he's gone at last'; the new baby takes over the
dead man's name.

So far the poem is explicit or almost so, but there are less
ponderable and yet potent influences discernible. The
layers of mist 'still persist', the mountains are like awakened
sleepers (sleep = death and resurrection) and there are
enumerations in several places, especially line 12, which
slow up the movement of the poem while adding a note of
regular certain revival as each 'unit' either comes into view
or bursts into song. Old John Thinn's terrific stretch of
memory is itself a stabilizing and slowing down factor; if
the new baby has a long life too, their combined span will
be long indeed.

7

For my part, if there is any way of getting a melancholy
satisfaction out of life it lies in dying, so to speak, before one is
out of the flesh; by which I mean putting on the manners of
ghosts, wandering in their haunts, and taking their view of
surrounding things. To think of life as passing away is a sadness;
to think of it as past is at least tolerable. (*Early Life*, p. 275)

[1] Richard Little Purdy, *Thomas Hardy, a Bibliographical Study* (London,
1954), p. 237. Cited as Purdy.

This represents an obvious desire to stand outside the flux; to observe, without participating and thus becoming involved in the wear and tear. He said that 'he preferred to be "the man with the watching eye" ' (*Later Years*, p. 246). It is, though present in a number of poems, usually either one inspiration among several or is modified by other considerations. It appears clearly in 'He Revisits his First School':

> After waiting so many a year
> To wait longer, and go as a sprite
> From the tomb at the mid of some night
> Was the right, radiant way to appear;
>
> (*Collected Poems*, p. 481)

to some extent in 'Afterwards', and in 'In Tenebris II'. (This 'set' of Hardy's mind could be responsible for much of Hardy's irony since the viewpoint of the *spectator ab extra* obviously encourages such an attitude.) I think that it is partly responsible for such poems as 'Let me enjoy' and 'To Life', where an attempt is made to extract a little happiness from life by a deliberate pretence that it is somehow different, and better than it is. Further examples, of varying degrees of obviousness, can be seen in 'My Cicely', 'The Bedridden Peasant', 'A Man' and 'The Shadow on the Stone'.

Close in inspiration to these are those poems which regard nostalgically the simple secure past, untroubled by thought and spiritual difficulties. There are other, and perhaps more immediate, reasons than a desire to arrest Time and therefore Mortality, but this desire would be active mainly at the subconscious level in any case. It appears openly in 'The Oxen', where the desire for the legend to be true is explicit —and pathetic:

> I should go with him in the gloom,
> Hoping it might be so.
>
> *(Collected Poems,* p.439)

Other examples can be found in 'Night in the Old Home', 'Afternoon Service at Mellstock' and 'Yuletide in a Younger World'. (I think that 'Afternoon Service at Mellstock' is too close to Hood's 'I remember, I remember' for the resemblance to be accidental, but this does not affect the argument above.) Another version, based on incidents in Hardy's boyhood, can be seen in 'In Tenebris III'.

I believe that this theme or influence or compulsion (it seems to have some of the characteristics of all three) could be traced further, and in some rather unlikely places, though this would lead us from literature to psychology. Two suggestions may give some indication of the possibilities. Readers of Hardy's novels have frequently noticed how often he begins with a solitary figure on a road or some similar scene. Journey poems, too, are not uncommon and the illustrations to *Wessex Poems* are worth noting as there are several which show this kind of scene or the similar one of a track crossing a deserted landscape.

In Gwendolen Murphy's anthology, *The Modern Poet*, Edwin Muir discusses his poem 'The Riders' and states that the poem is essentially about mortality and immortality. He continues:

I was not aware, or at least fully aware, of all these implications when I wrote the poem; and I have only realized during the last year that almost all my poems from the start have been about journeys and places: that is about the two sides of the paradox [of mortality and immortality] one of which implies the other. (pp. 168–9)

If Muir can write about immortality while ostensibly writing about journeys and not be aware of it, it does not seem unreasonable to wonder if Hardy is doing the same, though, unlike Muir, he had a number of modes of expression for his theme.

Hardy is fond of insisting that, so far as the visible world is concerned, 'man is the measure of things', e.g.

The poetry of a scene varies with the minds of the perceivers. Indeed, it does not lie in the scene at all.   (*Early Life*, p. 66)

An object or mark raised or made by man on a scene is worth ten times any such formed by unconscious Nature.
(*Early Life*, p. 153)

. . . the beauty of association is entirely superior to the beauty of aspect, and a beloved relative's old battered tankard to the finest Greek Vase.   (*Early Life*, p. 158)

Some handlings of this theme, such as 'The Seasons of her Year' and 'It Never Looks like Summer' are rather perfunctory, but 'A Wet August' is much better and 'On the Way' is a small but clear triumph; the grotesque imagery in each descriptive stanza emphasizes and deepens the strength of 'mind over matter' in the refrain stanzas. There are several possible reasons for being so insistent about this point and one of them could be a desire to make Man the centre of the Cosmos and, in fact, the only really active force in it. This is admittedly difficult to reconcile with some of his other ideas; for example, he said of the poems in *Moments of Vision* that

they mortify the human sense of self-importance by showing, or suggesting, that human beings are of no matter or appreciable value in this nonchalant universe.   (*Later Years*, p. 179)

But it is common property that Hardy was an unsystematic

thinker and quite capable of holding mutually contradictory views. Such poems as 'The King's Experiment', 'Alike and Unlike' and 'The Difference' show how the desire to impress the landscape with Mind and the realization that the Flux will continue can combine in a poem. Hynes points out another variation: 'One can see why the Return was an action which appealed to Hardy; it symbolizes man's efforts to reverse the movement of Time and to assert the present existence of the past' (p. 50). See for instance, 'The Revisitation' and 'Welcome Home'.

8

Hardy's sensitivity to the passage of Time seems to have been abnormal, but almost innate, for example:

> In those days the staircase at Bockhampton (later removed) had its walls coloured Venetian red by his father, and was so situated that the evening sun shone into it, adding to its colour a greater intensity for a quarter of an hour or more. Tommy used to wait for this chromatic effect, and, sitting alone there, would recite to himself 'And now another day is gone' from Dr Watts' Hymns, with great fervency, though perhaps not for any religious reason, but from a sense that the scene suited the lines.

(Early Life, p. 19)

It needs only common observation to see the effects of Time on Man and Things, but to most people their observations remain purely personal and casual; to Hardy, they fitted into a 'philosophy' and into the general trend of his thought. Probably no other writer has ever placed such emphasis on the fact that women grow old—and he did this at twenty-six, in the 'She to Him' sonnets!

> When you shall see me in the toils of Time,
> My lauded beauties carried off from me,

My eyes no longer stars as in their prime,
My name forgot of Maiden Fair and Free.

(*Collected Poems*, p. 11)

The same thought can be seen in 'Amabel', 'Former Beau-
ties', 'The Revisitation' and others. These gain in importance
and pathos when they are seen as the results and symbols
of an inevitably losing battle against Time and Mortality.
It is significant that almost all the poems which embody
this theme are concerned also with losing love, one of the
stabilizing factors in the flux.

Owing partly to his profession of architect and church
restorer, he seemed to think of the effect of Time as a
boring or abrading process:

as years gnaw inward . . . ('San Sebastian')

I feel him boring sly. ('In a Eweleaze near Weatherbury')

Delve sly to solve me back to clay. ('A Sign Seeker')

I say something about Hardy's observation of Time later,
but his sensitiveness to some of its effects seems to belong
with his feelings about Immortality.

On the whole, attention in this chapter has been concen-
trated on the themes of the poems rather than on the poems
themselves. The main purpose has been to indicate that
Hardy's few central ideas and interests influenced a large
number of his poems, that many of his 'quirks' are, or
could be, derived from these ideas and that most are a
reasonable following of a particular 'pattern in the carpet'
(itself of wider interest and less abnormal than is generally
assumed). Sympathetic understanding still leaves many
'bad' poems bad, but may alter one's opinion of some
apparent failures. As we have seen, critical assessments are

ludicrously at variance and this ought, if it does nothing else, to make us a little less dogmatic.

In the many contradictions and variations, we see an essentially simple, humble mind seeking for the light; sometimes by examining trifles, sometimes by speculations on a cosmic scale, but in either case seldom able to rest for long in any conviction and making poetry out of this inability, as in 'Nature's Questioning'.

> 'Or come we of an Automaton
> > Unconscious of our pains? . . .
> > Or are we live remains
> Of Godhead dying downwards, brain and eye now gone?
>
> 'Or is it that some high Plan betides,
> > As yet not understood,
> > Of Evil stormed by Good,
> We the forlorn hope over which Achievement strides?'
>
> Thus things around. No answerer I. . . .
> > > > (*Collected Poems*, p. 59)

Yeats has made the most enlightening generalization about such poems: 'We make out of the quarrel with others, rhetoric, but out of the quarrel with ourselves, poetry.'

V

Memory and Drama

HARDY's Trinity of time, memory and death are closely knit, but can perhaps be separated for closer inspection. His fascination with Time has been illustrated already, with some of its sources. When the idea of God or Guiding Providence disappears or becomes incredible, Time and Truth come to have a very close association. Truth instead of being part of the divine order is a revelation, perhaps a product, of Time. This, with Hardy, frequently results in a poem based upon a rather obvious, almost mechanical, juxtaposition, as in 'The Seasons of Her Year':

i

> Winter is white on turf and tree,
>   And birds are fled;
> But summer songsters pipe to me,
>   And petals spread,
> For what I dreamt of secretly
>   His lips have said!

ii

> O 'tis a fine May morn, they say,
>   And blooms have blown;
> But wild and wintry is my day,
>   My song-birds moan;
> For he who vowed leaves me to pay
>   Alone—alone!

(Collected Poems, p. 143)

Certainly, here, 'Truth is the Daughter of Time', but it is hard to claim that this particular truth is given poetic validity. The triteness of the truth is not relieved by any virtues of rhythm, imagery or language. It bears all the marks of one of Hardy's inventions which, as was seen in the previous chapter, rarely produce a good poem. 'Mute Opinion' is a parallel example; a political and historical 'truth' is involved instead of a personal one, but the poem is no more successful. When, as in 'Before and After Summer', this method is used to embody one of his ponderings instead of illustrating one of his whimsies, an attractive if not great poem results.

The importance of this theme and the variations upon it which Hardy produces can be seen in many poems; for instance, 'The Minute before Meeting', 'The Voice of Things' and 'He Abjures Love', besides many of the poems connected with Emma Hardy. These poems are often successful, I think, though at various levels. (It must be admitted that some of them attempt very little.) 'After Reading Psalms XXXIX, XL, etc.' is inspired by this theme too. Reading of it can produce very strong, and varied, reactions. It is, therefore, a fairly severe test of what he could make of one of his ruling ideas.

> Simple was I and was young;
>   Kept no gallant tryst, I;
> Even from good words held my tongue,
>   *Quoniam Tu fecisti!*
>
> Through my youth I stirred me not,
>   High adventure missed I,
> Left the shining shrines unsought;
>   Yet—*me deduxisti!*

At my start by Helicon
    Love-lore little wist I,
Worldly less; but footed on;
    Why? *Me suscepisti!*

When I failed at fervid rhymes,
    'Shall,' I said, 'persist I?'
'*Dies*,' (I would add at times)
    '*Meos posuisti!*'

So I have fared through many suns;
    Sadly little grist I
Bring my mill, or any one's,
    Domine, Tu scisti!

And at dead of night I call:
    'Though to prophets list I,
Which hath understood at all?
    Yea: *Quem elegisti?*'

                (*Collected Poems*, p. 660)

The oddness appears, before the reader has even started, in the painfully literal title; it is difficult to think of any other writer who would have written 'etc'. in such circumstances. A first reading discloses few attractions and much awkwardness. The rhyming seems forced and obtrusive, the language almost intolerably literary and the rhythm apparently unremarkable; the Latin evokes little response in the minds of most readers, apart from those who know their Dunbar. But out of this mish-mash, a poignant personal idiom has been created—poignant because personal, in that it has been created by the pressure of contemplation—out of the conviction that Truth has emerged from Time. The two previous poems were probably also the results of this, but there the conviction is less profound and less personal. In fact it is hardly exaggerated to say that the profundity of conviction *is* the poem.

Yet although profound conviction is the starting point of the poem, it is also generated as it proceeds. The first two stanzas are comparatively light and smooth; the third and fourth are more broken and have a wry tone. The last two have both smoothness and wryness while adding a passionate eloquence which, though it may have been latent in the very conception of the poem, has emerged in the process of contemplation and creation.

According to A. P. Elliott, the 'President of the Immortals' was 'Time the Arch-Satirist' in the first American publication of *Tess of the D'Urbervilles*, and the first sketch of *The Well-Beloved* was entitled 'Time Against Two'.[1] This is significant of the rôle of Time; it is a permanent underlying theme, but is so closely linked with other themes (or, perhaps, incompletely separated from them) that it seldom dominates in the finished work and can be expressed in terms of these other themes. It may, however, become a principle of structure. Thus, Hynes emphasizes what most readers must have noticed to some extent; that Hardy frequently 'organized his poems in temporal terms, rather than in spatial or logical forms' (p. 50). Examples of this can be seen in 'The Seasons of Her Year', 'Mute Opinion' and 'Before and After Summer' all referred to earlier.

The belief that Truth is the daughter of Time and will be revealed by it does not, in itself, necessitate or imply any particular kind of vehicle for the truth—there is no obvious reason for supposing that it cannot manifest itself in the trivia of daily life. Hardy was, notoriously, a great collector

[1] *Fatalism in Thomas Hardy* (Philadelphia, 1935), p. 74.

G

of such trivia and it is clear that he meditated on them and their significance; his interest in anniversaries and his re-handling of an incident (for example, in 'Childhood among the Ferns') indicate this. It is not suggested that he accumulated them for this pupose; merely that his temperament and convictions alike prompted him to use the material in this way.

This characteristic 'ritual' can be seen clearly in 'Near Lanivet 1872', which as I mentioned in Chapter I has been attacked as 'versifying an anecdotal experience that has been insufficiently subjected to the powers of imagination', but which is, I think, a magnificent justification of the theme and method.

Some incidents and facts will certainly continue to resist judgement or interpretation and will remain teasing and mysterious. It is not surprising that Hardy wrote poems on this kind of mystery, nor that they are of unequal value. 'The Sigh', for example, never rises above the peculiarity of the idea that gave it birth.

In 'Beyond the Last Lamp' we read a poem, flawed though it is, of a different and higher level, or, perhaps, with an additional dimension:

i

While rain, with eve in partnership,
Descended darkly, drip, drip, drip,
Beyond the last lone lamp I passed
　　Walking slowly, whispering sadly,
　　Two linked loiterers, wan, downcast:
Some heavy thought constrained each face,
And blinded them to time and place.

ii

The pair seemed lovers, yet absorbed
In mental scenes no longer orbed

By love's young rays. Each countenance
    As it slowly, as it sadly
    Caught the lamplight's yellow glance,
Held in suspense a misery
At things which had been or might be.

iii

When I retrod that watery way
Some hours beyond the droop of day,
Still I found pacing there the twain
    Just as slowly, just as sadly,
    Heedless of the night and rain.
One could but wonder who they were
And what wild woe detained them there.

iv

Though thirty years of blur and blot
Have slid since I beheld that spot,
And saw in curious converse there
    Moving slowly, moving sadly
    That mysterious tragic pair,
Its olden look may linger on—
All but the couple; they have gone.

v

Whither? Who knows, indeed. . . . And yet
To me, when nights are weird and wet,
Without those comrades there at tryst
    Creeping slowly, creeping sadly,
    That lone lane does not exist.
There they seem brooding on their pain,
And will, while such a lane remain.

                (*Collected Poems*, pp. 296–7)

As one would expect, this incident was almost certainly witnessed by Hardy himself; the poem was first published in 1911 and he had been living in Tooting (the poem is sub-titled 'Near Tooting Common') thirty years earlier. The original, trivial, incident becomes something substantial and gathers significance with each new stanza. One can see how this is done, up to a certain point, by an analysis of the language and details; for instance the rain and the evening, 'in partnership' like the mysterious couple, the monotony of the repetition of night and rain, the 'singsong' chime of each fifth line, the light which merely serves to display the sad faces. But the incident seems to rise to more than can be explained in this way, to the pitch where it has deep symbolic significance. I find it striking that the one point where the poem seems to me to 'wobble' is the beginning of the last stanza, the point farthest away from the details of the incident; and yet, perhaps, this is just what ought to be expected.

It has been remarked already that Hardy is very much the poet of Memory, a point emphasized by McDowall: 'Almost as much as Wordsworth he was a poet of Memory, that inmost medium of all that is continuous in the mental life' (p. 203).

As we have seen, the comparison with Wordsworth is very pertinent, and McDowall's reference to 'all that is continuous' is worth consideration too. Hardy depended on his memory to an outstanding extent, and it served him well, often over very long stretches of time. Walter de la Mare relates a conversation with Hardy, then in his eighties, about an incident at school which must have occurred seventy years earlier. Hardy was remorseful about this incident; indeed, with him, Remorse is a characteristic, almost inevitable, product of Memory, and, in turn, a very fruitful source of inspiration.

Frequently, even when the poem is of 'mixed' inspiration, the memory material is a very valuable part, as it is in 'At Middle-Field Gate in February'. The sensuous particularity of the first two stanzas makes them a fine piece of writing, but the poem is lifted to a higher level by the precise recollection of the last.

It is impossible to say what proportion of Hardy's output can be classified as Memory poems (for one thing, the term itself lacks precise definition), but it is a large one; reminiscence is one of his characteristic modes; '... the tone of an ageing man watching the fire die down and thinking of old tunes, old memories: moments remembered at railway stations and lodging houses: sunsets at the end of London streets, water coming over the weir, the rain on the downs' (Young, p. xxxii).

Even some of the exceptions are more apparent than real; for instance, he always tended to regard Napoleonic history as personal and local, since he had absorbed so much of it in his youth. Rome and pre-history frequently enter, but usually by way of their remains in Dorset. Otherwise, well-known historical or fictional characters or scenes are very rare, and he had no taste for the exotic:

Mrs. Hardy: 'We read his [Edward Shanks'] *Queen of China.*'
Hardy: 'Oh yes, I remember. It is not a title that would naturally interest one.'

(Collins, p. 7)

Thus, as we have seen, a kind of logical circle was formed; Hardy relied upon his memory; a great deal of his recollections consisted, as was to be expected, of trivia; his 'philosophy' allowed and encouraged him to regard this plentiful stock of trivia as significant; and very often he made good his claim.

The five Napoleonic ballads, all in *Wessex Poems*, are an interesting example of the effect which this 'memory habit' had upon poems not relying *primarily* upon memory for their inspiration. One poem, 'The Alarm', is based upon a family tradition and is therefore on a different footing from the others. The remaining four are not, as might be expected, simple narratives of exciting events, but a much later account of them, provoked, in three cases, by specific incidents; the remark about the daughter in 'San Sebastian', the playing of a particular tune in 'Leipzig', and the approach of death in 'The Peasant's Confession'. Hardy has provided for their stories his own kind of 'Wordsworthian' recollected inspiration; something which need not have been a memory has been made to look like one. (In 'Leipzig', this is achieved only at the cost of some rather clumsy explanation.)

The tendency to turn what is, or could be, 'contemporary' narrative into reminiscence is strange in view of Hardy's frequent claims to be a dramatic poet:

The pieces are in a large degree dramatic or personative in conception; and this even where they are not obviously so.

Preface to *Wessex Poems, Collected Poems*, p. 3

. . . the sense of disconnection, particularly in respect of those lyrics penned in the first person, will be immaterial when it is borne in mind that they are to be regarded, in the main, as dramatic monologues by different characters.

Preface to *Time's Laughingstocks, Collected Poems*, p. 175

The intervening book, *Poems of the Past and the Present*, had a similar claim in its Preface. Later volumes either had no Preface or enabled Hardy to carry on his chronic skirmishing with his critics over his 'philosophy'; there is no indication, however, that he ever abandoned his claim to be a dramatic poet, which raises several interesting points.

First, one suspects that Hardy had at least one strong motive for maintaining this, irrespective of its truth. It seems certain that despite his occasional expression of surprise at attacks on his philosophy, he knew that they were inevitable (see 'The Impercipient'). The claim that his poems were really the expression of an invented character, or of a different school of opinion, was an obvious, if crude, device for avoiding some of the odium. He was neither the first nor the last to use it. John Keble had realized, before Hardy's birth, that this method had its advantages:

But now remember that the whole tribe of lyrical poets (if that is the right name for them) cannot avail itself of this expedient of shifted responsibility, since in this species of poetry everything is uttered in the poet's own person.[1]

Hardy's comments on Barnes are also relevant:

Even if he often used the dramatic form of peasant speakers as a pretext for the expression of his own mind and experiences—which cannot be doubted—yet he did not always do this, and the assumed character of husbandman or hamleteer enabled him to elude in his verse those dreams and speculations that cannot leave alone the mystery of things—possibly an unworthy mystery and disappointing if solved, though one which has a harrowing fascination for many poets—and helped him to fall back on dramatic truth by making his personages express the notions of life prevalent in their sphere.[2]

---

[1] *Keble's Lectures on Poetry 1832–1841* (Oxford, 1912), trans. E. K. Francis, ii, 99.

[2] *Select Poems of William Barnes* (London, 1908), pp. xi–xii.

Hynes, who quotes this passage, suggests plausibly enough that Barnes's example was responsible for Hardy's preference for the dramatic form and that 'It satisfied Hardy's compulsive reticence' (Hynes, p. 27). What is, I think, more interesting is that Hardy seems to associate the dramatic form with some kind of evasion or escape. On this showing, Barnes's escape was more drastic since whole areas of thought were completely evaded, while Hardy dealt with them under the guise of a semi-fictitious personality. The section in parenthesis above certainly seems a personal confession as well as a general critical statement.

The attempt to consider how far Hardy *was* a dramatic poet leads immediately to questions of definition. One of the speakers in T. S. Eliot's 'A Dialogue on Dramatic Poetry' claims that the minor writers of the Greek Anthology, Martial, Homer and Dante, are dramatic. This is rather inclusive, but F. O. Matthiessen is probably interpreting Eliot's thought correctly when he says 'In the terms of such a description the dramatic element in poetry lies simply in its power to communicate a sense of real life, a sense of *the immediate present*—that is, of the full quality of a moment as it is actually felt to consist.'[1]

As we have seen, Hardy does attempt to communicate a sense of the immediate present in the sense that he tries to arrest the flux of Time and Change, but the connection between this and Matthiessen's concept is superficial; Hardy attempts to freeze the present rather than to make it actual. 'Continuous present' would be a better term and is, in fact, used, slightly modified, by Blackmur (p. 74). ('Hardy using it [refrain] to keep the substance of his ballads—what

[1] *The Achievement of T. S. Eliot, An Essay on the Nature of Poetry* (2nd ed. London, 1939), p. 66. Author's italics.

they are actually about—continuously present.') Indeed, Hardy's temperament seems to be at a great remove from this fundamental aspect of drama. His chief resource is memory and his chief modes, meditation and reminiscence. One feels that with him thought has long preceded words and has formed itself almost without them, that there has been brooding in almost inarticulate meditation upon Experience and experiences, and only later have the metrical moulds been formed to receive the results. The situation is precise and particular, but is given weight by the accumulation of past emotion and experience. The poem is not an attempt to re-create experience, but to say something about it (in the sense not of coming to a conclusion about it, but of discerning a quality in it). Take, for example, 'A Commonplace Day':

> The day is turning ghost,
> And scuttles from the kalendar in fits and furtively,
> To join the anonymous host
> Of those that throng oblivion; ceding his place, maybe,
> To one of like degree.
>
> I part the fire-gnawed logs,
> Rake forth the embers, spoil the busy flames, and lay the ends
> Upon the shining dogs;
> Further and further from the nooks the twilight's stride extends,
> And beamless black impends.
>
> Nothing of tiniest worth
> Have I wrought, pondered, planned; no one thing asking blame or praise,
> Since the pale corpse-like birth
> Of this diurnal unit, bearing blanks in all its rays—
> Dullest of dull hued Days!

. . . .

—Yet, maybe, in some soul,
In some spot undiscerned on sea or land, some impulse rose,
    Or some intent upstole
Of that enkindling ardency from whose maturer glows
    The world's amendment flows;

    But which, benumbed at birth
By momentary chance or wile, has missed its hope to be
    Embodied on the earth;
And undervoicings of this loss to man's futurity
    May wake regret in me.

                 (*Collected Poems*, pp. 104–5)

This is, I think, an example of a superficially dramatic appearance concealing a profoundly undramatic mood. The present tense and the precise 'immediate' description of the second stanza notwithstanding, the poem is the embodiment of meditations which have been forming themselves silently and gradually. It is not event, but event and understanding, completely integrated. The attempt to discern a quality in life has probably prevented any attempt to render character, or the *excitement* of experience. It is, I think, possible to combine all three in spite of the opinion of Yvor Winters, but he is probably right in asserting that the first tends to be obstructed by the other two.[1] Consciously or not Hardy realized where his real strength lay.

So far the results of the search for the dramatic have been negligible. I think that there is a special, limited, sense in which Hardy can be said to be a dramatic poet, but before discussing this, there are some minor points to be considered. The assumption and, therefore, the revelation of a character other than the author's own is something which Hardy

---

[1] Yvor Winters, *Edwin Arlington Robinson* (Norfolk, Conn. 1946), p. 23.

rarely achieves—probably rarely even attempts. 'Panthera' is as successful as it is because of a heavy reliance on Browning; and in any case, little character-revelation is attempted. The action is completed and is recounted rather than re-lived. It should also be noticed that there is a 'framework' to the main narrative, which is itself a reminiscence. It is, therefore, similar to the Napoleonic ballads which have been considered already.

Another problem is that posed by the fifteen 'Satires of Circumstance'. These have a high proportion of dialogue, are mostly in the present tense, are not meditative, and are obviously intended to create a vivid immediate impact. Some of them are fairly successful, for example, 'Outside the Window'. A reading of the fifteen, however, merely offers proof, if it were needed, that there is more to drama than those qualities. Obviously a group, they gain little by being so; they do not develop, but are merely extended. Anyone who doubts that Hardy's talent was for the meditative lyric should consider these poems.

One poem alone, perhaps, shows some indication of a talent for drama, 'At Wynyard's Gap'. The ironic situation is typical, but there is a light bitter-sweet touch which is not.

> HE: Yes: a mere matter of form, you know,
> To check all scandal. People will talk so!
> SHE: I'd no idea it would reach to this! (*Kisses him*)
> What makes it worse is, I'm ashamed to say,
> I've a young baby waiting for me at home!
> HE: Ah—there you beat me!—But, my dearest, play
> The wife to the end, and don't give me away,
> Despite the baby, since we've got so far
> And what we've acted feel we almost are!
>
> (*Collected Poems*, pp. 711–12)

The dialogue is better than Hardy usually achieved outside dialect, and the whole proves that Hardy's themes could be presented in a greatly transmuted tone and manner. It is, however, something of a sport—not bad, but not significant; it is plain that the author's strength does not lie here. The effect is similar to that produced by another idiosyncratic poet, de la Mare, when he attempst 'realism'. (There is one other poem, formally a drama, 'Aristodemus the Messenian', of which it is enough to say that I sometimes find it difficult to believe that it is not a parody.)

2

We have seen that one of the reasons for Hardy's claim to be a dramatic poet may well have been to shift the responsibility for his opinions on to the unspecific 'I' of the poems. It cannot be said that he usually achieves this; it is so obviously the poet himself speaking that, even if we believed Hardy was serious in his claim, most poems would still have that defect which Coleridge thought was typical of Wordsworth.

Either the thoughts and diction are different from that of the poet [rare in Hardy], and then there arises an incongruity of style; or they are the same and indistinguishable, and then it presents a species of ventriloquism. . . .

This can be seen in 'Nature's Questioning'. Not only is there no compelling reason why the natural objects should be speaking, but the ventriloquistic effect is strong since thought and style are pure Hardy. It is hard to say whether he was aware of this or not, since he could be very naive about such matters; the ill-suited language of 'The Peasant's Confession' seems even worse when Hardy excuses it on the ground that the peasant is speaking. Wordsworth, who offered a similar defence for ' The Thorn', at least preserved a more consistent linguistic level.

In the Preface to *Time's Laughingstocks* Hardy refers to his poems as 'lyrics penned in the first person' and as 'dramatic monologues', and this is a clue to the sense in which he is a genuinely dramatic poet, since there are occasions when poems can be both at once. In his Preface to *Cromwell*, Victor Hugo says that the romantic period is 'dramatic and therefore eminently lyrical'. Jacques Barzun, who quotes this, says that it has usually been accounted a paradox, but that it is not really so. He maintains that the romantic artist 'is in effect a dramatist using his own self as a sensitive plate to catch whatever molecular or spiritual motion the outer world may supply'.[1] A little further on he states that 'The lyricist is not always speaking for himself. He captures and reproduces the diverse, the conflicting essences of other beings .... The result is drama in the literal sense of con- flict and in the figurative sense of contrast' (p. 98). This is not applicable to Hardy without considerable qualification, but some poems of his have a quality which his reputation, or even a reading of much of his verse, would not lead one to expect, and the remark offers a hint concerning the origin and nature of this quality.

Few would disagree that many of the 'Poems of 1912–13', the 'Veteris Vestigia Flammae' group, are among Hardy's best. The claim that they are dramatic, and dramatic in a way which few of his other poems are, will probably be regarded as highly disputable; and yet I think that this is so. One of the finest is 'The Voice':

[1] *Romanticism and the Modern Ego* (Boston and London, 1943), p. 97.

Woman much missed, how you call to me, call to me,
Saying that now you are not as you were
When you had changed from the one who was all to me,
But as at first, when our day was fair.

Can it be you that I hear? Let me view you, then,
Standing as when I drew near to the town
Where you would wait for me: yes, as I knew you then,
Even to the original air-blue gown!

Or is it only the breeze, in its listlessness
Travelling across the wet mead to me here,
Your being ever dissolved to wan wistlessness,
Heard no more again far and near?

Thus I; faltering forward,
Leaves around me falling,
Wind oozing thin through the thorn from norward,
And the woman calling.

(*Collected Poems*, pp. 325–6)

There is no doubt that this seems to be the extreme point, or near extreme, of the personal lyric, but it is, I think, dramatic and impersonal also. We see the personal sorrow very acutely, but we see Sorrow almost naked, as a quality; not just Hardy's sorrow, but Sorrow itself. In Barzun's terms the sensitive plate has caught the spiritual motion which the outer world can supply. For many the feeling that this is so will be self-validating, but more impersonal arguments can be found to buttress this opinion.

If we compare the 'Veteris Vestigia Flammae' group with the great English elegies, 'Lycidas', 'Adonais', 'In Memoriam', one difference is immediately plain. Milton, Shelley and Tennyson were involved in a way that Hardy is not. They tend to move into discussion of themselves and their problems. *Their* fears, *their* hopes, *their* views of the universe are in the poems; but Hardy, who is supposed to thrust himself and his philosophy into his poems on every possible occasion, concentrates on his grief and loss. The poems are full of the pronoun 'I' and yet there is no obtrusive personality attached to it; the others are in fact both egoistical and personal, while Hardy is not, and the difference is not merely of degree. The quality of feeling is different. (There are several possible reasons for this; one, for instance, is that the other three poets were all young when they wrote.)

Milton and Shelley probably had little personal acquaintance with the man they mourned, but Tennyson had, and so the quality of this grief is worth considering. Tennyson's grief, like Hardy's, is exacerbated and deepened by the memory of shared emotions and experiences. Paul Verlaine gave as one of his reasons for failing to translate 'In Memoriam' that Tennyson 'had many reminiscences'. Hardy has, probably, even more, but his sorrow seems purer, deeper, more personal. And the difference lies, paradoxically, in Hardy's restraint, in his refusal to thrust himself into the poem.

The paradox rises to its height in the climax of one of his finest poems, 'The Going'. Here the lyrical-dramatic mixture has surely become an inseparable compound:

> Well, well! All's past amend,
> Unchangeable. It must go.
> I seem but a dead man held on end
> To sink down soon . . . O you could not know
> That such swift fleeing
> No soul foreseeing—
> Not even I—would undo me so!

> (*Collected Poems*, p. 319)

VI

Structure

IT is perhaps both courteous and sensible to allow Hardy himself to speak first:

Years earlier he had decided that too regular a beat was bad art. He had fortified himself in his opinion by thinking of the analogy of architecture, between which art and that of poetry he had discovered, to use his own words, that there existed a close and curious parallel, both arts, unlike some others, having to carry a rational content inside their artistic form. He knew that in architecture cunning irregularity is of enormous worth, and it is obvious that he carried on into his own verse, perhaps in part unconsciously, the Gothic art-principle in which he had been trained—the principle of spontaneity found in mouldings, tracery, and suchlike—resulting in the 'unforeseen' (as it has been called) character of his metres and stanzas, that of stress rather than of syllable, poetic texture rather than poetic veneer; the latter kind of thing, under the name of 'constructed ornament', being what he, in common with every other Gothic student, had been taught to avoid as the plague. He shaped his poetry accordingly, introducing metrical pauses and reversed beats; and found for his trouble that some particular line of a poem exemplifying this principle was greeted with a would-be jocular remark that such a line 'did not make for immortality'. (*Later Years*, pp. 78–9)

As with several of his remarks on poetry, this is interesting, but at first sight rather misleading. It is easy to get the impression that some far-reaching claims to literary innovation are being advanced, but the examples offered were nothing new and even if Hardy had used them more than he did, he would be at best an extender of rules rather than an innovator. Compared with Hopkins, Eliot and Pound, for instance, Hardy appears very traditional indeed (the true context of the quotation is almost certainly the kind or objection taken to Browning of 'want of melody and regularity'). The critics have fairly obviously been offended by the mixture of semi-conservative practice and vague revolutionary theory. (The wider public seem to have been less troubled and the schism, real or apparent, between the two was one of the starting points of this investigation.)

An additional complication enters because there is a feeling among critics that Hardy *ought* to have been an innovator in structure. They do not always make their adherence to this view explicit, but Hynes appears to hold it and, in any case, he puts the point clearly:

In discussing Hardy's style I suggested that this anti-formalist bias might be regarded as an aspect of Hardy's sense of his radical isolation from the intellectual and poetical tradition: if the traditional beliefs are dead, then the artistic process becomes a continual starting over. If this is true of Hardy's style, we might expect that it would also be true of the poetic forms he used— they should be personal and eccentric in something like the same way. (p. 74)

He goes on to point out that this does not normally happen.

Hardy's metres are basically traditional, while his stanzas, though very varied, are either common forms or modifications of them. The variety is admittedly very great— so great that Hynes refers to his inability to 'create a form which would transfer its excellences from one poem to another' and adds that 'Hardy went on to the end of his life trying again' (p. 88).

H

In fact we find the same mixture of truth, half truth and misunderstanding which we found when the 'philosophy' was discussed—and, as then, prejudice and insufficiently qualified assumptions are at least partly responsible.

One assumption has been mentioned already; that Hardy claimed to be an innovator and that the 'Gothic' quotation proves it. It is worth noting, however, that elsewhere he said that a poet could not hope to do anything new; he could only do what his predecessors had done, a little better.[1] He thus made two contradictory statements, both calculated to raise the hackles of sections of the public. In fact the contradiction is largely illusory. The claims of the 'Gothic' quotation are really fairly restrained; what is being expounded are the virtues of irregularity in detail against the background of a regular structure. (We need not consider how true this is of Gothic, since it is Hardy's view which is important here.) He is concerned with the *details* of decoration and structure, not with rebuilding or re-designing from the ground up. As with the 'philosophy', it is much more fruitful to think of him as at the end of one tradition than as at the beginning of another. (This might cause initial slackening of interest in Hardy, since as Eliot points out we are always inclined to favour writers who come at the beginning of an age and, since influence is a form of power, are impressed by a reputation for influence. He also says, however, that in the long run the matter is not relevant to our judgement.) The half-conscious belief of some readers that Hardy is a poetic revolutionary should be consciously and explicitly abandoned. Much disappointment will be avoided and the innovations that do exist can be appreciated.

[1] See page 11 above.

The second assumption is pervasive too, and is almost as difficult to pin down. It can be seen in the quotation from Hynes given above and is often expressed in some such form as 'a disordered age requires a disordered poem' (the contrary thesis that it requires an integrated poem would appear to be *logically* equally sound). With Hardy a disordered or disorientated individual or outlook is some-times substituted for a disordered age or world:

Chance rules Hardy's universe and it often seems to determine his style as well. And why, after all, in a lawless universe should there be laws governing poetry? Why *not* make poems out of clash-ing incongruities since this is the way the world is? (Hynes, p. 63)

Henry Adams comments in *Mont Saint Michel and Chartres* that 'Art had to be confused to express confusion; but per-haps it was truest, so'. Yvor Winters, who quotes this, remarks quite correctly that it is a variant of the doctrine of Organic Form;[1] and it is likely that this doctrine is at the bottom of some of the critical disappointment with Hardy. We are concerned here with modern manifestations of this doctrine—or dogma—and therefore it seems better to take a couple of more or less casual statements of it, rather than discuss its more 'philosophical' bases and histori-cal origins in Coleridge and Schelling:

. . . today the auditory rhetoric of a poem is dictated, not by its own rules, but by the central impulse of the poem.[2]

To impose arbitrary and external rules rather than to allow the artist's experience to mould [a poem's] organic form, is merely perverse.[3]

[1] *The Anatomy of Nonsense* (Norfolk, Conn., 1943), p. 163.

[2] Michael Roberts, *The Faber Book of Modern Verse* (London, 1936), p. 32.

[3] C. Levenson in *Delta*, Spring 1956, p. 8. (Quoted in John Press, *Rule and Energy* (London, 1963), p. 26).

It is difficult to refute this doctrine logically, as has been admitted by a better poet and critic than either Roberts or Levenson, Paul Valéry:

Freedom is so seductive, particularly to poets; it presents itself to their fancy with reasons that are so plausible and, most of them, well grounded; it clothes itself so suitably in wisdom and novelty, and urges us, by so many advantages whose dark side one hardly sees, to reconsider the old rules, judge their absurdities, and reduce them to the observance of the natural laws of the mind and ear, that at first one does not know what to reply.[1]

As Valéry hints, there are dark sides to the doctrine which can be exposed, such as the assumption of an exact equivalence between the experience and the poetic expression of it. (Another is to forget that concentration on technical matters can allow the imagination to work unhindered.) T. S. Eliot, who as poet has been one of the beneficiaries of the vogue of organic form, is very cautious about it:

It is misleading, of course, to speak of the material as creating or imposing its own form: what happens is a simultaneous development of form and material; for the form affects the material at every stage; and perhaps all the material does is to repeat 'Not that! Not that!' in the face of each unsuccessful attempt at formal organisation; and finally the material is identified with its form.[2]

The most *immediate* opposing argument, however, is the pragmatic one offered by Donald Davie in reply to Levenson. He pointed out that 90 per cent of poetry in the last five hundred years had been written in obedience to rules

---

[1] *The Art of Poetry* (London, 1958), p. 12.
[2] T. S. Eliot, *The Three Voices of Poetry* (London, 1953), p. 22.

and that 'it is in the nature of a rule to be external'.[1]

The correct deduction from all this seems to be that the supposed duty or necessity of writing in any kind of organic, expressive, 'disordered', or innovating form does not exist. This does not, of course, commit us to the belief that any poet is right in adopting traditional forms; merely that there is no *a priori* reason why he should not do so.

The reader soon becomes aware that the structure of Hardy's verse is usually regular and often elaborate. Technically he seems, frequently, to be making things as difficult for himself as possible. Outside *The Dynasts*, almost the whole of his verse rhymes, sometimes in complicated ways, and when the stanzaic pattern alters it is usually for some ascertainable reason. There is often a rigid and complicated stress pattern and marked variation in line length.

This elaboration can be observed easily enough in notorious cases. There are, for instance, the thirty-one 'me' rhymes of 'My Cicely', the twenty-nine 'ew' rhymes of 'The Flirt's Tragedy', the pantoum rhyme scheme of 'The Second Night', the triolets of *Poems of the Past and the Present*, and the heavy leonine rhyme of 'The Going of the Battery'. In addition, there are many poems in which the stanzas are rhyme-linked, again sometimes in complicated ways. Much of this is obvious even to the casual browser; closer inspection reveals more complexities, but it needs a reading of Dr Elizabeth Hickson's study, in which the information is given in concentrated form, to realize the amazing elaboration of the work as a whole.[2] The

---

[1] Donald Davie in *Delta*, Summer 1956, p. 27. (Quoted in Press, op. cit., p. 26).

[2] Elizabeth Cathcart Hickson, *The Versification of Thomas Hardy* (Philadelphia, 1931). Cited as Hickson.

elaboration is equalled by the variety of rhyme schemes; many are rare and some probably unique. According to Dr Hickson

Of the 916 poems listed we find only 141 which duplicate a metrical scheme used before, and on further study even these, in many cases, prove to be different because of the rhythmical variations introduced between the lines. (p. 50)

All this is, at first sight, rather surprising. The claim, explicit or implied, that some kind of organic form can be demanded of any poet has been rejected, but it is always open to a poet to create it—and Hardy is one of those whom we might expect to take advantage of this freedom; to this extent the assumptions of many critics are justified. In the matter of diction it is clear that Hardy was usually prepared to be exact and accurate at the cost of being very idio-syncratic; one might therefore expect similar or parallel idiosyncrasies in rhythm, rhyme and structure. They are not, *on the whole*, to be found, and this seems to need explanation; it must be admitted that a poet who combines a reputation for clumsiness with one for elaboration sounds awful.

Although the ultimate reasons for a poet's choice of a particular form are, and probably always will be, mysterious, partial elucidation is possible; much cannot be explained, but something can.

2

A persistent characteristic of his verse is the use of juxta-position; an event, opinion or scene is given and is followed by another which contradicts or substantially modifies the first, for example, 'The Comet at Yell'ham'.

i

It bends far over Yell'ham Plain,
    And we, from Yell'ham Height,
Stand and regard its fiery train,
    So soon to swim from sight.

ii

It will return long years hence, when
    As now its strange swift shine
Will fall on Yell'ham; but not then
    On that sweet form of thine.

(Collected Poems, p. 138)

This is a fairly obvious example; 'Mute Opinion', 'The Seasons of Her Year', 'On a Doorstep', 'It Never Looks like Summer' and many more are of the same type. Numerous poems such as 'The Convergence of the Twain' and 'The Wind's Prophecy' lack the clear juxtaposed *structure*, but are subtler versions of the same technique. It is, in fact, a form in which many degrees of elaboration, and success, are possible. Hynes calls this type 'antinomial' and regards it as Hardy's basic form. 'This characteristic structure can be demonstrated in virtually any one of Hardy's nine hundred odd poems' (p. 46). (It is difficult to reconcile this statement with the later one (p. 54) that 'as a criterion for judgement the antinomial pattern is generally a trustworthy one for dealing with Hardy'.)

It is obviously possible to see antinomial patterns everywhere if one has a mind to do so, though it means extending the term to cover oppositions and confrontations of many kinds and sometimes, in many ballad and narrative poems for instance, they are very hard to find. This difficulty could be eased by positing varying degrees of the pattern: it would, however, aggravate the difficulty that many poems in which the pattern is most obvious (e.g. Dr Hynes's own example of 'A Wife in London') are not very good.

It can be maintained that 'Hap', 'The Tramp Woman's Tragedy', 'Neutral Tones', 'Nature's Questioning', 'The Five Students', 'Afterwards', 'A Commonplace Day', 'In Tenebris', 'At Castle Boterel 'and 'To my Father's Violin', for example, are 'antinomial' poems. If they are all to be classified in this way, however, it is hard to find many that cannot; including 'If it's ever Spring Again', which Hynes specifically excludes (p. 70). The real weakness of the thesis, however, is that, even when relevant, it tends to turn a principle of structure into a principle of value. There are many degrees and kinds of success; I cannot see that the presence or absence of this kind of structure has the overwhelming influence which Hynes maintains it has.

It is, of course, a convenient and frequently used basis for a poem. (The almost perfect example, a very 'Hardyan' poem indeed, is Wordsworth's 'A slumber did my spirit seal'.) What I have called the juxtaposition poem is one, however, in which the structure is plain, the poem frequently consists of two stanzas or sets of stanzas and there is little attempt at resolution; the synthesis, if it occurs at all, is in the reader's mind.

Hynes is certainly right in thinking that the direct confrontation of thesis and antithesis in this way was often satisfying; for instance, 'Wives in the Sere'. There is at least one obvious reason which could go a long way towards accounting for the frequency with which Hardy writes a 'juxtaposition' poem (and, to some extent, poems of the looser 'antinomial' structure). His view of the Universe, as we have seen, was that of an essentially mindless, mechanical structure which was as likely to do one thing as another and the quality of whose acts was difficult or impossible to assess. Anyone taking this view may well acquire the habit of comparing one thing or opinion with another, and frequently coming to no decision at all about them.

If the writing of poems is based on this kind of philosophy and perception, two immediate consequences are probable. First, the obvious tendency will be to put the views in juxtaposed, identical forms, and, secondly, the intellectual purposes of the poem will be best served when this is done. The poetic value of 'The Seasons of Her Year', for instance, may be slight, but the poem has a point to make which would be greatly weakened if the second half were twice as long, or written in free verse. In fact we find, admittedly at a rather obvious level, just that connection between matter and form which some critics have denied that the poetry possesses.

A third consequence is that writing of such poems both needs and creates technical skill and that this skill, once acquired, is likely to become a tool to be used further for the pleasure of using it, sometimes in poems which gain nothing by it and where it draws too much attention to itself. This seems, at any rate, a possibility; it would be foolish to maintain more than that. Skill and pleasure in strict forms can be acquired in other ways and for other reasons; there is little doubt that such forms are congenial to many poets, some of them very different from Hardy. Eliot describes, approvingly, the methods of one of them:

A corollary, perhaps, of Valéry's emphasis upon the fundamental 'brainwork' . . . is his insistence upon the value for the poet of the exercise of difficult and complicated rhyming stanza forms. No poet was ever more conscious of the benefit of working in strict forms, the advantage to be gained by imposing upon oneself limitations to overcome. Such exercises are, of course, of no use to the man who has nothing to say . . .; but what they can teach the genuine poet, is the way in which form and content must come to terms.[1]

Eliot is here speaking of technical exercises rather than 'creative' work, but the distinction is often blurred, both in Valéry and poets generally. Thus, according to Valéry, speaking of his poem 'Le Cimetière Marin', '. . . . this intention was at first no more than a rhythmic figure, empty, or filled with meaningless syllables which obsessed me for some time' (op. cit. p. 148).

This is fairly close to Hardy's practice with verse skeletons, which some critics have been rather cool about. (Indeed, the view that poems should not be started in this way seems to be held by critics rather than poets and clearly depends upon the dogma of 'expressive form'.)

In earlier chapters, we have seen Hardy to be an uneasy, uncertain, obsessed man, unable either to solve his spiritual difficulties or to ignore them. It is hard to say what effect this kind of temperament will have on the form of a poet's verse, but it is possible that he will tend to use strict forms as a kind of foothold, a fixed point in an uncertain cosmos.

It is interesting to speculate on the relation between the strictness and musicality of a poet's form and his own anxiety. It may well be, I think, that the more he is conscious of an inner disorder and dread, the more value he will place on tidiness in the work as a *defence*, as if he hoped that through his control of the means of expressing his emotions, the emotions themselves, which he cannot master directly, might be brought to order.[2]

[1] Introduction to Paul Valéry, *Art of Poetry* (London, 1958), p. xiii.

[2] W. H. Auden, *Tennyson, An Introduction and a Selection* (London, 1946), p. xviii footnote.

This reminds us of Donne:

> I thought, if I could draw my paines,
> Through Rimes vexation, I should them allay,
> Griefe brought to numbers cannot be so fierce
> For, he tames it, that fetters it in verse.

and, to some extent, of Wordsworth's remark about the use of metre in restraining 'images and feelings [that] have an undue proportion of pain connected with them'. The possibility of a connection with Hardy's 'Keatsian' temperament, described in Chapter 3, is worth notice.

A more specific trait, which could have encouraged a desire for strict and perhaps complicated forms, is Hardy's obsession with time and his wish to arrest the flux, to halt 'the ongoing, i.e. the be-coming of the world' (*Early Life*, p. 265). He is fond, for instance, of rhyme-linked stanzas; one of the effects of this kind of structure is that the poem tends to seem closely joined and lacking in progression; in short, *static*, for example, 'Looking Across':

> i
> It is dark in the sky,
> And silence is where
> Our laughs rang high;
> And recall do I
> That One is out there.

> ii
> The dawn is not nigh
> And the trees are bare,
> And the waterways sigh
> That a year has drawn by,
> And Two are out there.

iii
The wind drops to die
Like the phantom of Care
Too frail for a cry,
And heart brings to eye
That Three are out there.

iv
This Life runs dry
That once ran rare
And rosy in dye,
And fleet the days fly,
And Four are out there.

v
Tired, tired am I
Of this earthly air,
And my wraith asks: Why
Since these calm lie,
Are not Five out there?

(*Collected Poems*, pp. 468–9)

The people in the poem are presumably Hardy and the members of his family; the poem is dated December 1915, which suggests that it was inspired by the death of his sister, Mary. The implications of the theme and the form are markedly at odds with each other. The substance of the poem is the undeviating, inevitable, progression to Death, those close to him being taken one by one. (This idea is handled in 'The Five Students', which occurs only seven poems earlier and may well have been written about the same time.) The structure, however, seems to have been designed, consciously or not, to allow very little movement. The twenty-five lines contain only two rhymes! which run through and link every stanza; in addition one of the b rhymes of each stanza, the last line, is identical (the last line is, in fact, a modified refrain). No less than ten lines begin with 'and' which—so to speak—adds, without chronological progression; this is quite apart from the effect of the mere repetition of the word itself. Furthermore, of the remaining fifteen lines, four begin with the same word 'that'. Individually these points may be trivial; collectively I think that they are significant. The consciousness of Time and Death produces, in the last stanza, apparent acquiescence; the structure of the poem tells a different, contradictory story.

This kind of structure is common enough in Hardy and analysis often produces similar results. As examples, chosen almost at random because they are printed next to each other, consider 'Evelyn G. of Christminster' and 'The Rift'. The method of linking and the themes are different, but there are obvious resemblances, particularly the 'binding' effect created by the linking. 'The Seven Times' and 'The Sun on the Letter' are worth examining as a kind of test case. The stanza-linking of the former seems justified by the theme, whatever one thinks of the ultimate value of the poem, but that of the latter seems an empty show of technical skill. The same method of linking—an unrhymed stanza which nevertheless rhymes with the next stanza is, I think, very effective in 'A New Year's Eve in Wartime', where it helps to create gradually a feeling at once terrifying and monotonous.

A similar effect can be obtained by the pattern of rhyming within the stanza. If it is intricate, the stanza tends to be bound together and static. A poem which consists of a number of such stanzas seems to have little movement, but to be a series of 'fixed' pictures.

> What seems it now?
> Lost: such beginning was all;
> Nothing came after: romance straight forsook
> Quickly somehow
> Life when we sped from our nook,
> Primed for new scenes with designs smart and tall. . . .
> —A preface without any book,
> A trumpet uplipped, but no call;
> That seems it now.

> *(Collected Poems, p. 595)*

This is the third stanza of 'A Two-Years' Idyll'. The rhyming pattern is intricate in the strict sense of the term; the echoes of the interweaving a and b rhymes seem suited to the reminiscent, pondering tone of the poem which looks back to what Hardy described as 'our happiest time' (*Early Life*, p. 156). One can well understand why he wanted to halt the passage of time here.

The 'closed-in', static nature of the stanza is emphasized by the repetition of the first and last lines (in the other two stanzas there is not even the slight one word variation found here). This use of repetition, semi-repetition and refrain is another of the stylistic traits of Hardy. Barnes had used it and Hardy, perhaps learning from him, employed it even more intensively. Technically it can be of many kinds; for instance:

> These flowers are I, poor Fanny Hurd,
> Sir or Madam,
> A little girl here sepultured.
> Once I flit-fluttered like a bird
> Above the grass, as now I wave
> In daisy shapes above my grave,
> All day cheerily,
> All night eerily!

—I am one Bachelor Bowring, 'Gent',
        Sir or Madam;
In shingled oak my bones were pent;
Hence more than a hundred years I spent
In my feat of change from a coffin-thrall
To a dancer in green as leaves on a wall,
        All day cheerily,
        All night eerily!
                                    (*Collected Poems*, p. 590)

and so on, with three lines repeating for a total of seven stanzas ('Voices from Things Growing in a Churchyard'). Sometimes the repetition/refrain echoes part of the previous line:

From Wynyard's Gap the livelong day,
        The livelong day,
                                    (*Collected Poems*, p. 182)

and so on for thirteen stanzas ('A Tramp Woman's Tragedy'). There is also the type seen already in 'A Two-Years' Idyll', which needs to be examined in a complete poem for its full effect to be appreciated. 'If You had Known' is an attractive example.

            If you had known
When listening with her to the far-down moan
Of the white-selvaged and empurpled sea,
And rain came on that did not hinder talk,
Or damp your flashing facile gaiety
In turning home, despite the slow wet walk
By crooked ways, and over stiles of stone;
            If you had known

            You would lay roses,
Fifty years hence, on her monument, that discloses

> Its graying shape upon the luxuriant green;
> Fifty years thence to an hour, by chance led there,
> What might have moved you?—yea, had you foreseen
> That on the tomb of the selfsame one, gone where
> The dawn of every day is as the close is,
> You would lay roses!
>
> (*Collected Poems*, p. 598)

He can obtain a similar effect with forms which seem too rigid to be anything more than jugglers' tricks. In 'A Leaving', refrain, repetition and identical but reversed line endings parallel the circuitous movement of the thought of the poem, obviously inspired by the funeral of Emma Hardy.

No one reason for the numerous examples to be found in Hardy's poems would be satisfactory. Some are obviously of the song and ballad refrain type ('A Trampwoman's Tragedy' is probably of this kind, though 'Tess's Lament', formally very similar, is probably not); some, for instance 'If You had Known', seem to be used for quite different reasons.

> . . . for the refrain—any agency at once iterative and variable about a pattern of sound—is a wonderful device for stretching and intensifying the process of sensibility. Hardy and Yeats are the great modern masters of refrain; Hardy using it to keep the substance of his ballads—what they are actually about—continuously present, Yeats using it to develop and modify the substance otherwise made present.   (Blackmur, p. 74)

Although Blackmur is here speaking of Hardy's ballads, the remark about keeping the substance 'continuously present' seems to be applicable to most of Hardy's devices of repetition. To keep something continuously present is to be very close to halting it; as we have seen, this is one of Hardy's emotional needs, and is, I suggest, one of the reasons for the complexity of his stanzaic forms.

Additional strength is given to this suggestion when we consider that Hardy's teacher in the matter of repetition may well have been Barnes, who disliked the whole process of change in his time, and that the poet associated by Blackmur with Hardy as a modern master of refrain was Yeats, another poet who hated the way the world was going.

3

So far the discussion has tended to exaggerate the strictness of form. As the 'Gothic' analogy shows, Hardy believed in the importance of minor irregularities, and numerous examples of irregularity and variety can be found easily enough. One class mentioned by Hardy, 'metrical pauses', is sparingly illustrated and 'reversed beats' not at all. Although they rightly occupied a great deal of Hardy's attention, it is doubtful if they should occupy much of the reader's, since he soon becomes acquainted with the most important consequence of their use, the cross-grained texture for which Hardy's poetry is well-known.

A good example of irregularity can be found at the end of 'The Going', quoted in the last chapter (page 99). Another already quoted is the fourth line of each stanza of 'Beyond the Last Lamp' (pages 86–87). The latter, since it is systematized, perhaps illustrates variety rather than irregularity; the same is true of the use of different rhythms and stanzas for different speakers, e.g. 'Heiress and Architect', or 'Haunting Fingers', where the speech is sharply differentiated from the narrative;

> 'O viol, my friend,
> I watch, though Phosphor nears,

I

And I fain would drowse away to its utter end
This dumb dark stowage after our loud melodious years!'

And they felt past handlers clutch them,
Though none was in the room,
Old players' dead fingers touch them,
Shrunk in the tomb.

(*Collected Poems*, p. 559)

'Leipzig', perhaps in imitation of traditional ballads, has several structural irregularities. Thus twenty-eight out of the thirty-six stanzas rhyme abab and represent the basic type; two of them, 9 and 35, have leonine rhyme in the first line. Seven stanzas, 6, 8, 17, 18, 19, 22 and 24, have end rhymes in the second and fourth lines only, but leonine rhyme in the first and third lines. In addition there is variation in line-length. The only marked tendency I can discern is that the variations are commonest about the middle; perhaps having interrupted his basic pattern, Hardy thought that he could then resume it. Another example is to be found in 'The Lost Pyx'.

I pointed out earlier that Hardy used refrain and repetition frequently and that they operate as a stabilizing factor. Effective variation or irregularity can be got by comparatively slight changes in the repetition itself, as in 'Overlooking the River Stour'.

This poem is, in inspiration, a product of the same period as 'A Two-Years' Idyll' and the function of the repetition of the opening and closing lines of each stanza is similar to that of the latter poem. In the final stanza, however, there is a fundamental shift in the thought of the poem as the comparative unimportance of the natural beauty is realized and this is paralleled by the change in the refrain.

Although his dialogue, other than rustic, is frequently ineffective, he often tries to approximate his rhythm to the speaking voice. This can be seen in 'In the Servants' Quarters' and 'The Man he Killed'; and, prominently, in 'Her Death and After':

> 'Forgive past days—I can say no more—
> Maybe had we wed you would now repine! . . .
> But I treated you ill. I was punished. Farewell!
> —Truth shall I tell?
> Would the child were yours and mine!'
>
> (*Collected Poems*, p. 35)

Hardy could, when he wanted, achieve a variety, at any rate, of organic form. A good, if unspectacular, example is to be found in 'Snow in the Suburbs':

> Every branch big with it,
> Bent every twig with it;
> Every fork like a white web-foot;
> Every street and pavement mute:
> Some flakes have lost their way, and grope back upward, when
> Meeting those meandering down they turn and descend again.
> The palings are glued together like a wall,
> And there is no waft of wind with the fleecy fall.
>
> A sparrow enters the tree,
> Whereon immediately
> A snow-lump thrice his own slight size
> Descends on him and showers his head and eyes,
> And overturns him,
> And near innurns him,
> And lights on a nether twig, when its brush
> Starts off a volley of other lodging lumps with a rush.

> The steps are a blanched slope,
> Up which, with feeble hope,
> A black cat comes, wide-eyed and thin;
> And we take him in.

> *(Collected Poems,* pp. 694–5)

The close observation is probably what strikes one first, but the structure of the poem and its rhythm are equally worth attention. In the first stanza the beginning and end represent more or less static conditions and the rhyming, particularly at the beginning, is obtrusive. The fifth and sixth lines imitate, or parody, the movement of the falling, upswirling snow. The second stanza is much lighter in rhythm. Here it is the fifth and sixth lines which contain the triple rhyme and are very short and tense. (A parody of the violent assault on the sparrow!) The last line describing a series of linked incidents is fittingly long.

The last stanza, quite different in form, has minimum description and business-like statement; thus ending a poem whose structure mirrors the movement of thought in a striking manner. There are other examples including 'The Sheep Boy', 'Fragment', 'A Light Snowfall after Frost', 'Bird Scene at a Rural Dwelling' and 'Not only I'. The last of these is an extreme example of go-as-you-please structure; rhyme, metre and line-length vary apparently at will. The beautiful patterns which the stanzas of 'The Pedigree' make on the page help to bring out the subtle variations and irregularities of the structure; this is even more obvious with 'A Spellbound Palace', a carefully wrought piece of description which all Hardy's critics seem to have overlooked. The high proportion of description among these poems is striking; when Hardy abandoned his characteristic 'philosophy-based' themes, he often abandoned strict forms too and wrote in a kind of semi-free verse.

One can easily balance the examples just given by others in which strict formality either enhances or creates poetic value (in addition, that is, to those, such as 'If You had Known', which were discussed earlier). Readers of 'Friends Beyond' have never, to the best of my knowledge, considered its structure, other than to remark on the *terza rima*'s being combined with a very short second line. There is, however, more than this; the twelve stanzas though not quite symmetrical are nearly so. The first three stanzas are narrative and the fourth and fifth a chorus of all the speakers. William Dewy has one line of the sixth stanza and the Squire the other two. Lady Susan has the seventh to herself. Farmer Ledlow has the first two lines of stanza eight and his wife the third (thus reversing the pattern of stanza six). Two stanzas in chorus follow. The spoken parts are perfectly symmetrical, the length of individual speaker's parts being apparently determined by their social standing! There are only two narrative stanzas at the end, so the second part of the poem just fails to be a mirror image of the first.

Hardy is, I think, one of the few poets, until very recent times, who have managed to write in the recognized very strict forms without being trivial. There are several triolets and a villanelle ('The Caged Thrush Freed and Home Again') in *Poems of the Past and the Present* which could be quoted as examples. They are often about birds; so in order to avoid suggestions (probably unjustified) of sentimentality the reader should consider 'How Great My Grief' (*Collected Poems*, p. 125) as a test case.

A poem which shows the possible advantages of both formality and variousness is 'One Ralph Blossom Soliloquizes'.

After a wry, informative prose epigraph the poem begins

> When I am in Hell or some such place,
> A-groaning over my sorry case,
> What will those seven women say to me,
> Who, when I coaxed them, answered 'Aye' to me?

By the fifth stanza, without alteration in metre, the tone has changed from low-keyed prosiness to

> Says Patience: 'Why are we apart?
> Small harm did you, my poor Sweet Heart!
> A manchild born, now tall and beautiful,
> Was worth the ache of days undutiful.'

So far the change has been a gradual ascension. Finally the stanza is extended and the rhythm made more subtle, but the polysyllabic rhyme retained:

> And Anne cries: 'O the time was fair,
> So wherefore should you burn down there?
> There is a deed under the sun, my Love,
> And that was ours. What's done is done, my Love.
> These trumpets here in Heaven are dumb to me
> With you away. Dear, come, O come to me!'
>
> (*Collected Poems*, p. 271)

A similar 'rise', without structural change, can be seen in 'Long Plighted' and 'Reminiscences of a Dancing Man'.

4

The objection that in over 900 poems there are likely to be exceptions to, and variations upon, anything has some justification, and it is certainly true that Hardy usually preserves a set structure. There are the usual critical disagreements about the value of doing so. Southworth, who seems to have paid more attention to this than most critics, has his doubts:

> The greatest obstacle to the poet's successful communication, however, lies in his frequent attempts at enclosing the thought in a predetermined pattern, ill-fitted for the purpose. (p. 166)

(The objection here, it should be noted, seems to be to ill-fitting fixed patterns, not to fixed patterns themselves; but no critic seems to separate the two concepts for long.) Hynes makes a similar comment (p. 75). Southworth's examples, omitting objections to individual lines, are 'Often when Warring', 'In a Wood', 'The Young Churchwarden' ('a borderline case'), 'An Anniversary', 'St Launce's Revisited', 'Quid Hic Agis', 'On a Midsummer Eve', 'The Re-Enactment', 'To my Father's Violin', 'News for Her Mother', 'At a Seaside Town' and 'The Musical Box' (pp. 166–8). (It is only fair to point out that the objections are not quite the same in each case.) One of Southworth's weaknesses is, I think, a tendency to scan first and then be troubled by the resultant difficulties; for instance,

> 'An Anniversary' presents difficulties of scansion. It contains iambs, anapests, amphibrachs, third paeons, and at least one trochee. The pattern is difficult because it gives no sense of being inevitable, nor is it readily discernible even after several readings.' (p. 167)

Much of this may well be true, but disagreement on the exact stressing has not prevented several people agreeing with me that this is a fine poem, and I have heard at least one very satisfactory 'professional' reading on the 'Third Programme'.

Of the other examples, I agree, more or less, about 'St

Launce's Revisited', 'Quid Hic Agis', 'News for Her Mother' and 'At a Seaside Town'. The second is, I think, spoiled by its metre; it could be argued that the others never had anything to spoil. I disagree sbout 'The Young Church-warden', 'The Musical Box' (strongly!), 'On a Midsummer Eve', 'In a Wood' and, to some extent, 'The Re-Enactment'. The last, as Southworth hints, is a difficult case; it is probably true that the 'beat of the stanza' is too 'dog-trotty,' but it can be subdued by careful reading and the poem is good enough to make the attempt worthwhile. I disagree completely about 'To my Father's Violin', which I have always considered to be a fine poem and I am glad to find that I have the support of Dr Hickson. She, like Southworth a metrical expert, quotes the whole of it as an example of how 'by skilful use of medial cesurae and logical enjambement, differing in every line, the stanzas are made to appear very different in structure' (pp. 36–8). This kind of contradiction would be astounding if one did not soon become hardened to it when reading Hardy's critics; here the cause can, I think, be discovered. Southworth is probably scanning to the exclusion of everything else; hence, he has failed to notice how the jerky movement is subtly fitted to the turns of the recollecting mind.

Thus, at least one reader has failed to be convinced by two-thirds of Southworth's examples, chosen, it should be remembered, from over 900 poems. My own first choice would have been 'The Master and the Leaves', not mentioned by him at all.

That Hardy does fail in this way is generally agreed, but it is much harder to get agreement on specific cases, which may indicate that they are less common than appears at first. Southworth, in fact, notices this:

Hardy rings such a multitude of changes within the course of a few pages that the fault in communication often lies in the reader's unconscious permission of the intrusion of mnenomic irrelevances, and not in any deficiency of the poet. Time after time, for example, I have made jottings about poems containing prosy lines, rhythms without subtlety, crowded lines, too faint stresses and so forth, only to find on further reading that I disagreed with my earlier impressions. (p. 167)

The moral here is too obvious for comment.

Perverse and misdirected ingenuity seldom result in any-thing except an uneasy feeling that someone who should know better is making an exhibition of himself. One does feel this about Hardy, sometimes. It probably would have been better if 'My Cicely' and 'The Flirt's Tragedy' had been less spectacular in rhyming; if, again, he did not some-times flog an idea to death, as in 'So Various' (an uncon-sciously ironic title). But he succeeds far more frequently than he fails; and the failures are, granted Hardy's poetic temperament, probably the price paid for the skill which so often integrates form and manner without diminishing accuracy or overthrowing rhythm.

'To Meet, or Otherwise', for instance, is a typical Hardyan theme encased in a typical Hardyan complicated form; less obvious but equally typical are the changes of tone and movement within it. Here are stanzas 2 and 3 :

> Yet I will see thee, maiden dear, and make
> 　　The most I can
> Of what remains to us amid this break
> 　　Cimmerian
> Through which we grope, and from whose thorns we ache,
> 　　While still we scan
> Round our frail faltering progress for some path or plan.

By briefest meeting something sure is won;
　　It will have been:
Nor God nor Demon can undo the done,
　　Unsight the seen,
Make muted music be as unbegun,
　　Though things terrene
Groan in their bondage till oblivion supervene.

(Collected Poems, p. 292)

Stanza 2 flows on its gentle, winding, slightly ponderous way, interrupted only by a couple of parentheses. Stanza 3 starts in a sharper, firmer, semi-epigrammatic fashion, making an obvious, though not obtrusive, contrast to the previous 'tune' which it modulates back into towards the end. Stanza 3 may owe a little to Browning's 'The Last Ride Together':

Look at the end of work, contrast
The petty done, the undone vast,

but this simply proves that Hardy could digest his influences properly.

Southworth remarks that 'mnenomic irrelevances' from the reading of other poems of Hardy interfere with understanding. It is even worse to have preconceived ideas of what is, or is not, suitable for certain types of poem. Miss Helen Darbishire says of Wordsworth's poem 'The Russian Fugitive' that, besides other defects, it is in a metre 'that would be the undoing of any serious poem'.[1] Both the metre and stanza of this poem are the same as those of Hardy's 'The Darkling Thrush,' which, so far as I know, has never been held to lack seriousness.

Starting with the right expectations or, at any rate, not

---

[1] *The Poet Wordsworth* (Oxford, 1950), p. 66.

with wrong ones, is always important, but particularly so with a type of poem found mainly in *Poems of the Past and the Present*. This volume was published at the end of 1901; the first part of *The Dynasts* (finished 1903) was probably being written at the same time as some of the shorter poems (see Purdy, p. 122), and in the Preface Hardy has an interesting passage on a possible way of rendering certain kinds of poetry:

In respect of such plays of poesy and dream a practical compromise may conceivably result, taking the shape of a monotonic delivery of speeches with dreamy conventional gestures, something in the manner traditionally maintained by the old Christmas mummers, the curiously hypnotizing impressiveness of whose automatic style—that of persons who spoke by no will of their own—may be remembered by all who ever experienced it. (*The Dynasts*, Wessex Edit., p. xii)

Many of the *Poems of the Past and the Present* have obvious 'philosophical' connections with *The Dynasts* (say, 'The Mother Mourns' and 'The Subalterns'). Some of them seem to be more effective if they are rendered in the manner described above, 'a monotonic delivery'; for example, 'The Lacking Sense', 'The Problem' and 'The Bullfinches'. A stanza from the first of these shows the typical movement of this stylized genre:

O Time, whence comes the Mother's moody look amid her labours,
As of one who all unwittingly has wounded where she loves?
Why weaves she not her world-webs to according lutes and tabors,
With nevermore this too remorseful air upon her face,
        As of angel fallen from grace?
                              (*Collected Poems*, p. 106)

This style is undoubtedly suited best to 'philosophical' expositions, but at least one other poem, 'Tess's Lament', seems to belong here; possibly because its rather weary, defeated, tone approximates it to them:

5

So far this discussion has not touched the centre of the matter. Hardy, contrary to what one might expect, has chosen to write his poetry in fairly rigid forms. What is the effect of this on his best work, the work in which we feel the real, the bed-rock Hardy? What, in this kind of poetry, are the advantages which can be gained from the limitations? Some help can be got from a very interesting account of two types of poetry given by Owen Barfield:

> Another test is this: it is much harder to convey the *full* effect of poetry of the architectural type with the *voice*. The eye seems to be necessary as well, so that the sense of a whole line or period can be taken in instantaneously. The actual sounds have grown more fixed and rigid and monotonous; the stresses accordingly are more subtle, depending on the way in which the emotional meaning—as it were—struggles against the rigidity; and this produces a movement different indeed, but none the less lovely because it is often audible only to the inward ear. The fluid type of verse, on the other hand, is made for reciting or singing aloud and probably gains more than it loses by this method of delivery.[1]

It is obvious that this is relevant enough to Hardy to warrant closer attention. A point in which it may be felt that there is a difficulty is the opposition of this type of poetry to song, since nearly all critics have commented

[1] Owen Barfield, *Poetic Diction* (2nd ed. London, 1952), p. 99. Author's italics.

upon the musical background and inspiration of much of his poetry; for example: 'He was steeped in the ancient music of rural England, of song and dance, of psalm and hymn; of village choir and of harvest home: and the example of William Barnes was there to show him what could be made of it' (Young, p. xii).

Despite this, I feel that the musical inspiration, in its more obvious forms at any rate, was not always a source of strength and plays a minor part in his better, personal, verse. He was, indeed, very interested in folk song, 'filling up leisure moments not by anything practical, but by writing down such snatches of the old country ballads as he could hear from aged people' (*Early Life*, p. 110). 'Reminiscences of a Dancing Man' is a tribute to another form of music, 'Lines to a Movement in Mozart's E Flat Symphony' to a third, 'I Knew a Lady' a fourth, and 'Sine Prole (Mediaeval Latin Sequence-Metre)' yet another.

But the third and fifth of these are more or less isolated experiments; the first produced charming but rather slight poems such as 'Timing Her' and 'O, I Won't Lead a Homely Life', while the fourth is the inspiration of that unfortunate type of which, as was noted, Blunden remarks 'the word Song prefixed to an item is to be considered as a warning that what follows will not be in Hardy's strongest way of sense or fancy'. He instances such verse as 'Her Apotheosis (Faded Woman's Song)', 'In the Street (Song)', 'Known had I (Song)', 'As 'twere Tonight (Song)', 'He inadvertently Cures his Love-pains (Song)' and so on, which I consider to be Hardy's worst work. He says that he studied folksong as a kind of hobby and much of the verse obviously 'musically' inspired reads like the output of a poet with time to pass, but nothing particular to pass it with.

Hardy may well have thought that this was what he could, and should, do; his remark in old age that 'the model he had set before him was "Drink to me only", by Ben Jonson' (*Later Years*, p. 263), does seem to indicate a desire and expectation of excelling in song. But I think that emphasis upon the musical inspiration of his verse is a mistake, which clouds the issue generally and tends to hide the true sources of his greatness. His best work seems to support strongly the opinion that the 'music' of poetry is *absolutely* different from that of music itself.

A point which may seem not to be relevant, but possibly is, is Barfield's statement that 'the eye seems to be necessary as well, so that the sense of a whole line or period can be taken in instantaneously'. This is true of Hardy, perhaps, more so than most poets. Poets whose work shows care, other than that of printer's routine, in arrangement on the page tend to belong to the 'avant garde'. Readings of Hardy soon suggested to me that some special care had been taken, an opinion later strengthened by a reading of McDowall.

> You cannot turn over a volume without noticing the exactness and varieties of the pattern on the page. Something more, of course, is implied in this than the inessentials of printing, though the verses have a very meticulous arrangement of that sort.   (McDowall, p. 249)

John Crowe Ransom, discussing 'The Subalterns', also draws attention to the importance of the appearance of the poem on the page.

It is hard to say exactly what effect this arrangement has on the reader (an effect which is greatly lessened by the more economical typography of the Collected Edition). Good examples, however, can be seen if the following are read in the original edition of *Moments of Vision*; 'To my

Father's Violin', 'The Figure in the Scene', 'The Tree and the Lady', 'The Pedigree' and 'The Ballet'. It can perhaps best be described as forcing the reader to realize that there is a *complicated* pattern here, and yet encouraging him by assurance that there *is* a *pattern*. He is therefore forced, as Barfield says, to take in wholes at once, and to proceed slowly, as is almost always necessary when reading Hardy. Despite occasional 'jewels', he is not a one line poet.

When what I have called the real bed-rock Hardy is considered, we find a form, half lyric, half meditative, in which the voice seems both to obey and defy the underlying structure. As Barfield says '. . . the stresses accordingly are more subtle, depending on the way in which the emotional meaning—as it were—struggles against the rigidity'. Barfield is speaking generally, but it is difficult to find a poet whom the remark fits better than it does Hardy. Many poems, pondering, revolving, 'architectural', get their characteristic tone—and it is very characteristic—from this tension. The way in which the thought runs with the rhythm *and* clashes with it embodies the work of a mind forming its thought slowly and painfully, but precisely. If the rigidity lessens, the tension slackens; provided that sufficient 'pull' can be generated the greater the rigidity the greater the tension.

It would be easy and pleasant to deal with numerous examples: 'After the Last Breath', 'A Commonplace Day', 'To my Father's Violin', 'The Souls of the Slain' (where this movement is subdued to narrative); 'On One who Lived and Died where he was Born', 'At Castle Boterel' (which shows the emotional potency of spare statement); 'In a Eweleaze near Weatherbury' (a poem in which the emotional meaning is struggling against an apparently too

flowing rhythm) and 'To an Unborn Pauper Child'.
The last poem is one which nothing less than full quotation
can do justice to:

i

Breathe not, hid Heart: cease silently,
And though thy birth-hour beckons thee,
Sleep the long sleep:
The Doomsters heap
Travails and teens around us here,
And Time-wraithes turn our songsingings to fear.

ii

Hark, how the peoples surge and sigh,
And laughters fail, and greetings die:
Hopes dwindle; yea
Faiths waste away,
Affections and enthusiasms numb;
Thou canst not mend these things if thou dost come.

iii

Had I the ear of wombèd souls
Ere their terrestrial chart unrolls,
And thou wert free
To cease, or be,
Then would I tell thee all I know,
And put it to thee: Wilt thou take Life so?

iv

Vain vow! No hint of mine may hence
To theeward fly: to thy locked sense
Explain none can
Life's pending plan:
Thou wilt thy ignorant entry make
Though skies spout fire and blood and nations quake.

v

Fain would I, dear, find some shut plot
Of earth's wide wold for thee, where not
    One tear, one qualm,
    Should break the calm.
But I am weak as thou and bare;
No man can change the common lot to rare.

vi

Must come and bide. And such are we—
Unreasoning, sanguine, visionary—
    That I can hope
    Health, love, friends, scope
In full for thee; can dream thou'lt find
Joys seldom yet attained by humankind!

                    (*Collected Poems*, pp. 116–17)

No two of these six stanzas have the same movement,
though none deviates very far from the underlying pattern.
Frequently the corresponding lines move in different ways
(for instance, the first line of each stanza). Sometimes
when, as at the end of stanza 4, it seems that a smooth
movement is developing, a dragging line halts it (here, the
last one).

Form and Manner are truly one; it is often so and when it
is, then the form the poet adopts is so truly his that it does
not seem possible that it could have been different. Hardy's
structure is then as suited to him as Miltonic blank verse to
Milton and the couplet to Pope.

VII

Vocabulary

As the examination of vocabulary has often been made difficult, and the results misleading, by the separation of words and lines from their context and ambience, the starting point, at any rate, should be quotation and discussion of a poem long enough to show some typical categories and usages.

A Sign Seeker

I mark the months in liveries dank and dry,
    The noontides many-shaped and hued;
    I see the nightfall shades subtrude,
And hear the monotonous hours clang negligently by.

I view the evening bonfires of the sun
    On hills where morning rains have hissed;
    The eyeless countenance of the mist
Pallidly rising when the summer droughts are done.

I have seen the lightning-blade, the leaping star,
    The cauldrons of the sea in storm,
    Have felt the earthquake's lifting arm,
And trodden where abysmal fires and snow-cones are.

I learn to prophesy the hid eclipse,
    The coming of eccentric orbs;
    To mete the dust the sky absorbs,
To weigh the sun, and fix the hour each planet dips.

I witness fellow earth-men surge and strive;
    Assemblies meet, and throb, and part;
    Death's sudden finger, sorrow's smart;
—All the vast various moils that mean a world alive.

But that I fain would wot of shuns my sense—
    Those sights of which old prophets tell,
    Those signs the general word so well
As vouchsafed their unheed, denied my long suspense.

In graveyard green, where his pale dust lies pent
    To glimpse a phantom parent, friend,
    Wearing his smile, and 'Not the end!'
Outbreathing softly: that were blest enlightenment.

Or, if a dead Love's lips, whom dreams reveal
    When midnight imps of King Decay
    Delve sly to solve me back to clay,
Should leave some print to prove her spirit—kisses real;

Or, when Earth's Frail lie bleeding of her Strong,
    If some Recorder, as in Writ,
    Near to the weary scene should flit
And drop one plume as pledge that Heaven inscrolls the wrong.

—There are who, rapt to heights of trancelike trust,
    These tokens claim to feel and see,
    Read radiant hints of times to be—
Of heart to heart returning after dust to dust.

Such scope is granted not to lives like mine. . . .
    I have lain in dead men's beds, have walked
    The tombs of those with whom I had talked,
Called many a gone and goodly one to shape a sign,

And panted for response. But none replies;
No warnings loom, nor whisperings
To open out my limitings,
And Nescience mutely muses: When a man falls he lies.

(*Collected Poems*, pp. 43–4)

The reader of Hardy soon comes to expect almost any mixture of language, but this poem shows a freedom above even his norm.

Some of the usages have been put in tabulated form for ease of reference.

Heavy alliteration: e.g. 'I mark the months in liveries dank and dry', and almost the whole of the fifth stanza. It does not seem to be fulfilling any specific purpose.

Rare words: 'subtrude', 'inscrolls'. The only authority quoted for the intransitive use of the former in the O.E.D. is this poem. The only quotation for 'inscrolls', except this passage, is *The Merchant of Venice* (ii. vii. 72).

Archaic—dialectal—literary: 'wot', 'the general', 'mete', 'moils'. However one classifies these, they are certainly remote from normal usage.

Unusual forms: 'solve' (dissolve); 'limitings' (limitations).
Unusual affix-constructions: 'outbreathing', 'unheed'.

Simplicity: 'I have lain in dead men's beds, have walked/ The tombs of those with whom I had talked'.

One could go on further and point out that the vividness of 'earthquake's lifting arm' and 'leaping star' contrasts with the vagueness of 'noontides many-shaped and hued'; that the deadness of 'warnings loom' contrasts with the felicity of 'negligently' and 'hissed'. There is also the fondness for personification; 'King Decay' and 'Nescience', the latter an invention of very doubtful value. The original version had 'trancéd' for 'trancelike'; and 'to lives like mine' was 'my powers indigne' (Hardy's revisions, as we shall see later, frequently removed some peculiar usages while leaving many more). The most amazing thing is that the poem is an impressive one and is not sunk by such a verbal hodge-podge.

Hardy's successes and failures in this field have attracted a fair amount of critical attention and the comments have usually been sensible. Thus, William Archer, referring specifically to 'The Peasant's Confession', said that Hardy sometimes seemed 'to lose all sense of local and historical perspective in language, seeing all words in the dictionary on one plane, so to speak, and regarding them all as equally available and appropriate for any and every literary purpose' (quoted in Blunden, p. 104). Blunden makes a similar comment: 'it does not matter to Hardy whether others would have given these words a ticket of admission or not' (p. 265); McDowall refers to his style as an 'amalgam' (p. 205).

The basic reasons for Hardy's choice of vocabulary are, like those for his choice of structure, certain to remain unknown. This is normal, but additional difficulty is created by Hardy's few recorded comments, which are occasionally helpful, but sometimes misleading. His most serious effort, an attempt to correct and elucidate Wordsworth on poetic diction, seems to me neither clear nor enlightening and to have little connection with his own practice (*Later Years*, p. 85). A better start can be made by considering Hardy himself, instead of his opinions.

'. . . long years of absolution from criticism must needs be paid for in faults of style. 'Writing for the stage,' Mr Meredith himself has remarked, 'would be a corrective of a too-incrusted scholarly style into which some great ones fall at times.' Denied such a corrective, the great one is apt to sit alone and tease his meditations into strange shapes, fortifying himself against obscurity and neglect with the reflection that most of the words he uses are to be found, after all, in the dictionary.'[1]

Here, we clearly have an intensifying factor. Whatever *created* Hardy's linguistic mélange, his late start as a published poet might have strengthened it. With trivial exceptions, no verse was published until he was fifty-eight. Although he wrote it from youth, he made no sustained attempt at publication, nor did he seek advice as he did about the writing of novels.

Hopkins is, perhaps, a special case among Hardy's contemporaries, but an interesting parallel is offered by Doughty, also a late starter as a published poet and also very idiosyncratic in vocabulary. Some of Hardy's peculiarities were smoothed out when he was publishing verse regularly and he sometimes took heed of the criticisms of reviewers, but the 'amalgam' persisted, in a modified form, to the end of his life.

It is plain that a poet's use of language, conscious and unconscious, will be mainly determined by his upbringing, education, tastes, amusements, experiences, profession, social milieu and by the complicated reactions and stresses between them. Hardy's diction can therefore be studied, to a considerable extent, in categories suggested by his biography. This will not contradict what was said earlier about the importance of context, since at this point we are concerned with the sources of the diction and how it was formed, not with the more important matter of how it was used when formed.

[1] Walter Raleigh, *Style* (London, 1897), pp. 67–8.

2

Hardy seems to have been annoyed by the suggestion that he was a peasant, and a dialect-speaker; he was, indeed, neither, but he was familiar with the Dorset dialect and lived for much of his life among people to whom it was the normal method of communication and of whose life it was an adequate expression. He defended both its use and its right to existence on several occasions and knew what was at stake, but obviously realized that the cause was lost; that industrialism and universal education would kill the Dorset dialect just as the railway had killed the traditional ballads (*Early Life*, pp. 25–6). Robert Graves tells a story which shows how far this process had gone.

I remember that when I stayed with Thomas Hardy in 1920 he complained to me: 'Yesterday I was not sure of a rustic word which I wanted to use in a poem, and once again found myself at a loss: because the only authority quoted for it in the *Oxford English Dictionary* was my own *Under the Greenwood Tree*, 1872.'[1]

The future of a dialect is very uncertain indeed when one of its leading advocates has to obtain support from dictionaries. In fact, an examination of the poems shows that, as frequently with Hardy, the practice is not what one would expect from the theory. Dialect is employed much less than one would suppose, and in rather limited circumstances. Apart from one whole poem, 'The Bride-Night Fire', and the dialogue of four or five more, it occurs almost entirely in single words. The list given by Dr Hickson consists of only 137 words (and this includes such unimportant variants from standard English as 'pu'pit', 'a'most' and 'pa'son'.

[1] Robert Graves, *The Crowning Privilege* (London, 1955), p. 196.

Of the 137, 36 occur in 'The Bride-Night Fire' and 16 in 'Valenciennes'. A poet who uses 85 dialect words in over 900 poems is hardly a dialect writer in any serious sense.

This is not the whole truth, of course; Hickson herself points out that many of the 150 words she classes as obsolete were probably in use in Wessex (p. 73); and the 'archaic' and 'rare' categories would supply some examples too. (Critics who have objected to 'kine' and 'treen' as obsolete ought to consider how far they were obsolete to Hardy.) In addition there are some usages which she has failed to detect at all; for instance, while = until: '. . . while the true one forth-come' ('The Temporary the All') and starving = freezing: 'And a few leaves lay on the starving sod' ('Neutral Tones').

'The Bride-Night Fire' is an early experiment in full dialect, unfortunately not repeated. 'Valenciennes' and 'The Curate's Kindness' are monologues in dialect, and it is used also for the dialogue in 'The Homecoming' and the humbler speakers of 'Friends Beyond'. The object here is obviously realism; the speakers would, in real life, use dialect. Then there are words which are, strictly speaking, dialect, but which Hardy probably regarded as normal, e.g. linhay, leaze, withwind. The mark of this kind is that it can be used in non-dialectal contexts without drawing much attention to itself. Some words are classed as dialect solely because they do not occur in standard English, though it lacks any equivalents for them, e.g. skimmer-cake. Hardy regarded the preservation of such words as one of the important functions of dialect:

The process is always the same: the word is ridiculed by the newly taught; it gets into disgrace; it is heard in holes and corners only; it dies; and, worst of all, it leaves no synonym.

(Preface to *Select Poems of William Barnes*, p. iii)

Some dialect words are plainly for special occasions or help to obtain special effects; for instance, to imply endurance or continuity:

'Yonder a maid and her *wight*' ('In Time of the Breaking of Nations'; *Collected Poems*, p. 511)

'For, *wonning* in these ancient lands' ('On an Invitation to the United States'; *Collected Poems*, p. 100)

Some words are probably used because they fit in with Hardy's evident dislike of separate adverbs which are intimately connected with their verbs, e.g. 'overgot', 'withinside', 'therence'. Metrical or rhyming convenience plays its part, e.g. 'The pale mews *plained* below us, and the waves seemed far away', ('Beeny Cliff') and

> Low murmuring: O this bitter scene,
> And thrice accurst horizon hung with gloom!
> How deadly like this sky, these fields, these *treen*.
> ('The King's Experiment'; *Collected Poems*, p. 149)

It should not be forgotten that Hardy's early environment was not only rural and dialectal, but included a rural and dialect poet. William Barnes was both poet and philologist, wanting the English language to be revived and purified by fresh grafts from its original Germanic roots. Some of his suggestions, such as 'pushwainling' for perambulator, have been laughing-stocks for a century, but most of his inventions were, if sometimes strange, logical enough. One of his principles seems to have been that the invention of new words or importation of dialect words into the standard language could be defended by analogy.

... but with a stronger or weaker, or a rougher or smoother expulsion of the breath, and thence they are called cognate or kinsletters.

A footnote to 'kinsletters' adds 'A Compound for which we have an authority in the words Kinsman and Kinsfolk'.[1]

Our useful adjectives ending in *some*, German *sam*, as *quarrelsome*, *noisome* . . . naming the state of a noun likely or given to do an action, would have been well taken into the national speech from any dialect in which they might be found, instead of those borrowed from the Latin; as *heedsome*, attentive; *winsome*, likely to win or captivate; *lovesome*, disposed to love; *blithesome*, disposed to be blithe; *fadesome*, *laughsome*, *runsome* (as mercury), *meltsome* (as butter or lead).[2]

Barnes has, as his definition of tmesis, the following:

A word-cutting or splitting or outsundering; as, 'The child has *overthrown* the flower-pot'. By word-cutting or outsundering— 'The child has *thrown* the flower-pot *over*'.
> 'By Tmesis you may oft outshare
> A word's two word-stems here and there.'[3]

As can be seen from his vocabulary in this very definition, Barnes seems to be using a form of Anti-Tmesis, keeping together parts of words which are usually separated; and, indeed, elsewhere in the same book he advocates this.

Why should not English, like other tongues, more freely form words with headings of case-words as *downfalls*, *incomings*, *offcuttings*, *outgoings*, *upflarings* instead of the awkward falls-down, comings-in, cuttings-off, goings-out, flare-ups; or *offcast* (for cast-off) clothes; or a *downbroken* (for a broken-down) schoolmaster; *outlock* or *outlocking* (for a lock-out); the *uptaking* beam (for the taking up beam) of an engine? (p. 43)

---

[1] *The Elements of English Grammar* (London, 1842), p. 10.

[2] *A Grammar and Glossary of the Dorset Dialect*. Published for The Philological Society (Berlin, 1863), p. 24.

[3] *An Outline of English Speechcraft* (London, 1878), p. 81.

Much of this sounds like Hardy (compare 'outbreathing' and 'unheed' in 'A Sign Seeker' above); if we associate the remarks on analogy with the implicit dislike of tmesis, we see a probable source of many of Hardy's unusual affix-constructions. For instance:

> with a calm *unruth*
> Cast eyes on a painter-youth. ('The Caricature')

> One who, past doubtings all,
> Waits in *unhope* ('In Tenebris I')

> I'd have my life *unbe* ('Tess's Lament')

> Taking his life's stern stewardship
> With blithe *uncare*. ('Four in the Morning')

In Dr Hickson's classification 'unruth' is archaic, 'unhope' obsolete, 'unbe' rare and 'uncare' coined: but such allo-cations, based on the O.E.D., are purely formal; it seems improbable that Hardy made any meaningful distinction between, for instance, the preservation of 'unruth' and the invention of 'uncare'; it is more likely that both are attempts to extend his linguistic command by analogy. He would feel all the more comfortable for knowing that the procedure had the approval of Barnes, who was a friend, master and colleague, as well as a philologist.

It is, of course, true that this 'anti-tmesis' was and, to some extent, still is one of the resources of the English language. The following are some of the examples noticed in the course of normal reading.

... Montrose stood on the Corbie Hill watching the *ongoings* in the town. (John Buchan, *Montrose*)

They were *upraised* in the days 'when men knew how to build'. (Jerome K. Jerome, *Three Men in a Boat*)

We are arranging to *uplift* this load within the permitted time.
(a commercial letter, 1959)

Examples from poets, for example, Wordsworth, Shelley and Keats are fairly easy to find.

The frequency of this type of word in Hardy is unusual, however. The only poet, since Anglo-Saxon times at any rate, who approaches it is Doughty. This is, I think, significant since the two poets seem to have worked quite independently, though the aged Hardy had apparently read *Mansoul*. Doughty was, of course, consciously attempting to return the English language and English poetry to old paths and old roots. His technique for this included the use of archaic, dialect and obsolete words; 'anti-tmesis'; and frequent compounds (as did that of another 'philological' poet, Hopkins). Anne Treneer remarks that—'he found it hard to resist compounds' and that 'he hated words which merely indicate relationship without meaning anything in themselves'.[1] The result is often bizarre.

> I looking up,
> Beheld the WAGGONER, now much wheeled downforth,
> Amidst the Signs . . . .
> . . . . She casts to Earth;
> Sailing through holt of heaven, whilst Earthlings sleep:
> All other radiance lies on heaths night-breast;
> Sheepwolds, where ploughman never clave the turf.
> Where the great bustard timbers, from Mans foot,
> Remote, her rough-built solitary nest.[2]

This is not at all like Hardy and yet shows many of his

[1] Anne Treneer, *Charles M. Doughty: A Study of his Prose and Verse* (London, 1935), p. 253.
[2] Charles M. Doughty, *Mansoul* or *The Riddle of the World* (2nd ed. London, 1923), pp. 194–5.

linguistic habits, e.g. *anti-tmesis*: downforth; *compounds*: night-breast; *archaisms*: holt, clave; *obsolete words*: timbers (= builds).

We have seen that Hardy's dealings with ideas rarely resulted in his theories being pushed to their logical conclusions and that he seemed largely unconscious of some of his own mental habits. Taking this into account, it seems reasonable to regard Hardy as a rather tentative, half-conscious, wanderer in the territory through which Doughty strode boldly. He is prepared to use dialect/rare/archaic/poetic words, though not as frequently as one might expect; by anti-tmesis, he reduced the number of 'words which merely indicate relationships without meaning anything in themselves'; he was a frequent user of compounds, without being able to achieve striking effects from them. (Bernard Groom describes him as 'another poet who uses compound epithets freely, but often without the transforming touch of poetry. Intent on the meaning he has to convey, he regards the compound epithet as a device for compression, or a useful metrical expedient'.)[1]

What we can probably learn from this is that Hardy, like Doughty, felt some dissatisfaction with the existing poetic language and that the precepts of Barnes seemed to offer an opening in the right direction. Owing to his incapacity for rigorous thinking, other literary influences, and the varying, hesitating, provisional quality of what he had to express, no real *new* style developed. A new style would have been analogous to a chemical compound; what actually emerged was a mixture, which is of varying composition and whose original constituents can be distinguished.

[1] Bernard Groom, *The Formation and Use of Compound Epithets in English Poetry from 1579*. S.P.E. Tract No. XLIX (Oxford, 1937), pp. 317–18.

3

It has frequently been pointed out that Hardy was largely self-taught and that autodidacts are notoriously prone to show off their knowledge—the rather contrived references to painters in *The Mayor of Casterbridge* have been quoted as examples. Hardy's learned words (for instance, 'subtrude' in 'The Sign Seeker') are often regarded as a product of this variety of display.

This suggestion is one which would command more assent if it were put forward more sympathetically and did not have an air of snobbishness. Hardy received full-time education until the age of sixteen, which was more than three-quarters of the population were getting a century later! The implication seems to be that anyone who has not been to public school and university has not been educated at all.[1] Hardy does not seem to have felt himself to be deprived or inferior, despite his being the author of *Jude the Obscure*. He did, it is true, study philosophy and a number of languages and did not push these studies to any great depth; as a result it is quite plausible to assume that the knowledge so gained never became an everyday part of him, but was regarded as something a little glamorous and prestigious. Some of his vocabulary seems to support this assumption.

> But now is as a gallery portrait-lined,
> And scored with *necrologic* scrawls.

('In a Former Resort after Many Years'; *Collected Poems*, p. 666)

> Waking but now, when leaves like corpses fall,
> And saps all *retrocede*.

('The Last Chrysanthemum'; *Collected Poems*, p. 136)

[1] This point is made by Raymond Williams in *Critical Quarterly*, vi (1964), pp. 341–2.

To where the daysprings well us
Heart-hydromels that cheer.

('I Worked no Wile to Meet You'; *Collected Poems*, p. 574)

It is possible that these words are not subdued to their surroundings and easy to believe that Hardy's education had not made him sensitive to such clashes, but much more difficult to make a convincing case against their use.

Even a casual reader of Hardy's verse might guess that he had been an architect and was interested in dancing and music, particularly folk music, since there are many references to, and terminology drawn from, these arts. The abundance of settings in churches and graveyards, partly the result of his professional frequenting of them, has been considered earlier. Their effect on vocabulary seems quite normal. The musical inspiration has also been considered; to summarize, this was considerable but not always fortunate and, so far as the better work is concerned, minor.

What the casual reader might not realise is the extent of Hardy's knowledge of English poetry. At one time he decided that since 'in verse was concentrated the essence of all imaginative and emotional literature' he would read verse only. 'And in fact for nearly or quite two years he did not read a word of prose, except such as came under his eye in the daily newspapers and weekly reviews. Thus his reading covered a fairly large tract of English poetry' (*Early Life*, p. 64).

He never attempted the discipline of systematic criticism and it is not likely that this mixture of mental puritanism and debauchery was ultimately good for his talent; less ground covered, but with greater thoroughness, would have equipped him better. The literary echoes and the rather stale poetic vocabulary which sometimes choke the poems probably owe a great deal to this period.

Some usages need a very charitable reader indeed.

> 'Thwart my wistful way did a damsel saunter.
>
> ('The Temporary the All'; *Collected Poems*, p. 5)

> When her spoused estate ondrew,
> And her warble flung its woo
>   In his ear.
>
> ('The Maid of Keinton Mandeville'; *Collected Poems*, p. 534)

> Thence to us came she, bosom burning,
> Welcome with joyousness returning.
>
> ('By Henstridge Cross at the Year's End'; *Collected Poems*, p. 595)

The general picture, therefore, is of a poet who had been subjected to a wide range of linguistic influences without any one of them having a chance to become dominant. This simply solves, to some extent, the question of origins—why Hardy possessed this varied vocabulary and his tendency to operate on varied linguistic and literary levels. Discussion of origins is usually interesting and, in this case, informative, but is secondary to other matters; how Hardy handled his vocabulary, what effects he tried to obtain, how far he succeeded, and how such a mixture could be transmuted into a genuine poetic language.

4

It has been pointed out in an earlier chapter that Hardy, though a poet of 'mixed' inspiration, inclined normally towards the 'Worsdworth' type, and that one of the marks of this type is the primacy of subject. The subject is something which has to be described or rendered, not created.

Sometimes, in both Hardy and the young Wordsworth, one can see traces of a belief that the event itself is more poetical than any literary account of it, the writer's task being to set down the event 'raw'.

However exalted a notion we would wish to cherish of the character of the Poet, it is obvious, that, while he describes and imitates passions, his situation is altogether slavish and mechanical, compared with the freedom and power of real and substantial action and suffering.[1]

This doctrine is basically anti-literary, and probably no poet could hold it for long and remain a poet. Wordsworth always qualified it by praise of the great potentialities of the poet, and a great deal of his later career can be construed as a continuous retreat from the advanced position thus taken up. In the above extract, for instance, 'his situation is altogether slavish and mechanical' was later changed to 'his employment is in some degree mechanical', a significant softening of the original proposition. In Hardy such poems as 'On Stinsford Hill at Midnight', 'In the Days of the Crinoline' and 'The Husband's View' seem to be of this kind; attempts to make the raw oddities of existence into literature.

This is, of course, an extreme position and the usual consequences of 'Wordsworthian' inspiration tend to emphasize words strongly. The experience has to be rendered as exactly and truthfully as possible; the prime virtue is accuracy and the most important linguistic level, that of meaning.

It follows from this position that first, the demands of accuracy may conflict with those of linguistic decorum; and

[1] William Wordsworth, *Lyrical Ballads with Pastoral and Other Poems*. 2 vols. (London, 1802), i, xxx.

L

secondly that there will be a tendency to think that accuracy is enough. The imaginative creative leap which makes the really great poem, the outstanding line, will be rather rare.

5

Hardy in his discussion of Barnes says: 'In his aim at close-ness of phrase to his vision he strained at times the capacities of dialect, and went wilfully outside the dramatization of peasant talk.'[1] Several critics have noticed the relevance of 'closeness of phrase to his vision' to Hardy himself, but the whole sentence is interesting, since Hardy did with English in general what Barnes did with dialect; he strained the capacities of any one level of it and went wilfully outside the dramatization of the utterance of any particular speaker.

One of the words against which specific objection has been made is 'stalk' in 'In Time of the "Breaking of Nations" ':

> Only a man harrowing clods
> In a slow silent walk
> With an old horse that stumbles and nods
> Half asleep as they stalk.

> *(Collected Poems*, p. 511)

The word 'stalk', however, raises a question in the reader's mind. It is good enough, but whether or not it is exactly the picture the poet had in mind is debatable. It satisfies the need of rhyme and of alliteration on 's', but does it not over-intensify the scene?   (Southworth, p. 153)

It is not clear exactly what Southworth's objection is, but plainly the fitness of the word is being questioned. The

[1] *Select Poems of William Barnes*, p. ix.

relevant definition in the O.E.D. runs 'to walk with stiff high steps like a long-legged bird, usually with disparaging notion implying haughtiness, sullenness, indifference to one's surroundings or the like. . . . In dialect uses the prevailing sense is one of awkwardness'. If Southworth consulted the O.E.D., perhaps the mention of the long-legged bird bothered him. Apart from this, it would be difficult to find any definition more to the point. The ploughman has a half-asleep horse which stumbles; perhaps half-asleep himself, he moves slowly and silently. We hardly need the dictionary to tell us that 'awkwardness' is one of the prevailing senses (dialect usages are usually relevant in Hardy). Furthermore, as the point of the poem is the emphasis on the independence and persistence of love and work, the basic things of life, amid catastrophic events, the meaning 'indifference to one's surroundings' seems as fitting as anything could be.

Mr Southworth's remarks about rhyme and alliteration are reasonable enough, but these play here, as frequently, a less important part than appears at first sight; they are usually subordinated to meaning and although excessive alliteration is one of Hardy's weaknesses, it is unsafe to *assume* that they have forced the choice of any word. The following example is from very early work:

> Numb as a vane that cankers on its point,
> True to the wind that kissed ere canker came:
> Despised by souls of Now, who would disjoint
> The mind from memory, making Life all aim.
>
> (*Collected Poems*, p. 13)

'Disjoint', though not classified by dictionaries as rare, seems to have only its past participle, disjointed, in common use. The natural inclination is to assume that the needs of rhyme are responsible for its presence here, but this is by no means certain. The image is based on that stiffest, straightest and most 'directional' of things, a weather vane; as 'Life' is to be forced to aim in a different direction, the implications of breaking or dis-membering something straight and rigid found in 'disjoint' seem fitting. Consider also 'The Discovery':

> I wandered to a crude coast
> 　　Like a ghost;
> Upon the hills I saw fires—
> 　　Funeral pyres
> Seemingly—and heard breaking
> Waves like distant cannonades that set the land shaking.

> And so I never once guessed
> 　　A love-nest,
> Bowered and candle-lit, lay
> 　　In my way,
> Till I found a hid hollow,
> Where I burst on her my heart could not but follow.

> (*Collected Poems*, p. 313)

After pausing for a moment to agree with anyone who points out that 'crude' has an alliterative function, we should observe how it works in the poem as a whole. The poem refers to Hardy's Cornish courtship (this piece of outside knowledge must be imported into many poems to gain full understanding). The coast is crude in the sense of natural, raw, virtually untouched by man, unrefined in the strict sense. The domestic scene in the second stanza (perhaps too coy) does, however, force forward the other general meaning of crude; rough in manners and civilisation. The reader does not have to make any choice since the two, though separate, pull in the same direction.

Perhaps the principle which ought to guide investigations of this kind can now be made explicit:

From this it follows that criticism of a poet's locutions should be inseparable from study of the context in which they occur. The question of the diction of poetry is a question of how words affect and are affected by the artistic contexts they enter.[1]

This is, of course, a counsel of perfection; in the first place words *will* carry with themselves connotations and over-tones from their use outside any particular work; and in the second, it cannot, in any case, be carried out on a large scale; provisional judgements *have* to be made by any sane reader. What it should prevent is the habit, frequent among Hardy's critics, of giving long lists of odd words, phrases or lines, as a treasury from which future additions to *The Stuffed Owl* can be drawn. Mrs Nowottny points out that '.... poetry has the extreme peculiarity of being able to raid other forms of language at will, taking from them as much or as little as it chooses and doing what it likes with the bits' (p. 42). Subject to the warning about the persistence of connotations, this represents a reasonable position; it is, at any rate, superior to the theory, which seems more tenacious than one would have thought possible, that there are words fit for English poetry and words which are unfit.

Two examples of what appear to be indefensible usages are 'brume' in 'The Contretemps' and 'senior soul-flame' in 'The Souls of the Slain'. Both poems are fairly long, and therefore the context is hard to reduce to a reasonable compass.

> A forward rush by the lamp in the gloom,
> And we clasped, and almost kissed;

[1] Winifred Nowottny, *The Language Poets Use* (London, 1962), p. 32.

> But she was not the woman whom
> I had promised to meet in the thawing *brume*
> On that harbour bridge; nor was I he of her tryst.
>
> (*Collected Poems*, p. 551)

'Brume', though not classified as rare, certainly is so, and the need for a rhyme to 'gloom' and 'whom' was obviously pressing. The important thing, however, is what part the word actually plays in the completed poem. It is unwise to insist strongly on the attraction of rare words, though this is not negligible; at any rate their use has the approval of Aristotle.

Deviation from the ordinary idiom makes diction more impressive; for, as men are differently impressed by foreigners and their fellow citizens, so are they affected by styles. Hence we ought to give a foreign air to our language; for men admire what is far from them.

'The Contretemps', however, tells a very odd story indeed, even by Hardyan standards. The mist which reduces visibility has its function in the story—the unusual situation almost demands an unusual word; the ending of the story is left in deliberate obscurity like the mist in which it began; I think it can be claimed that 'brume' at least focuses attention on this. (I admit that I cannot see any particular reason for the use of brume in 'Joys of Memory'.)

> Then, it seemed, there approached from the northward
> *A senior soul-flame*
> Of the like filmy hue.
>
> (*Collected Poems*, p. 85)

All previous examples have been words which are ultimately, I believe, a source of strength to the poem; here we have a weakness. The beginning and end of this poem are both magnificent; the description of Portland Bill, an elemental place for the discussion of basic verities, the symbolism of the line of longitude (unfortunately not clear since Hardy omitted the prose note which accompanied the poem on its first, periodical, publication); the Pentecostal symbolism which has been present throughout, because the poet in the first stanza is obviously awaiting a revelation; the impressive, final, mass 'suicide'. In the body of the poem, however, Hardy tries to make the significance of his vision explicit, and much of it seems 'manufactured' in the worst sense of the word. We must feel, for instance, that these 'sprites without mould' are human and yet impalpable, so he uses 'soul-flame'. They have to be authoritatively informed of something; Hardy evidently wishes to keep the military and avoid the Christian hierarchy, so 'senior' is used. The fact that the result, 'senior soul-flame', is ludicrous to many tastes bothers him not at all. He has said *succinctly* what he wanted to say.

The partial failure to embody the initial vision or inspiration, and thereby to re-create it in the reader, is seen in other poems, such as 'On the Esplanade', 'The Shiver' and 'His Heart'. (It is of course a defect of 'Wordsworthian' inspiration: Coleridge, noting it in Wordsworth, called it 'mental bombast'.) Other interesting examples can be seen in 'The Place on the Map', where the connection between the map and the speaker's mental turmoil is never really brought to life, though Hardy often does this kind of thing well; and 'Jubilate', which just fails to be the very impressive poem it should be, with its amazing vision of the Dead dancing in their transparent graveyard.

> Through the shine of the slippery snow I now could see,
> As it were through a crystal roof, a great company

Of the dead minueting in stately step underground
To the tune of the instruments I had before heard sound.[1]

(*Collected Poems*, p. 480)

Words which seem at first to belong to the wrong
linguistic level often turn out to be what is needed, e.g.

When we as strangers sought
Their *catering* care,

('At an Inn'; *Collected Poems*, p. 60)

and:

A frail moan from the martyred saints there set
Mid others of the erection
Against the breeze, seemed sighings of regret
At the ancient faith's rejection
Under the sure, unhasting, steady stress
Of Reason's movement, making meaningless
The *coded* creeds of old-time godliness.

('A Cathedral Façade at Midnight'; *Collected Poems*, p. 667)

Alliteration, again, probably played its part in the selection
of these words, 'catering' and 'coded'. Yet I suspect that
behind their selection is the feeling that accuracy and brevity
count before all else. They have both, in addition, their part
in the organization of the poem. 'At An Inn' begins at
comparatively low emotional tension and rises in a cres-
cendo:

O severing sea and land,
O laws of men,
Ere death, once let us stand
As we stood then!

[1] This is, in structure, a memory poem and it is worth noting how the
'framework' is made deliberately drab and vague to highlight the vision.

'Catering', concise, but flat, almost commercial, starts the poem off prosaically enough for the 'rise' to be gradual but considerable. This 'rise' is, as we have seen (p. 122), one of Hardy's characteristic structures. 'Catering' is certainly not the first word which came into Hardy's head. The MS of *Wessex Poems* has 'sheltering' erased, but not replaced. 'Catering' was evidently inserted at a late stage.

'Coded', on the other hand, is a small terse link in a long, stately, yet concentrated, verse sentence—the tinge of disdain introduced by it, though faint, is perceptible.

> They've a way of whispering to me—fellow-wight who yet
> abide—
> In a muted, measured note
> Of a ripple under archways, or a lone cave's *stillicide*.
>
> ('Friends Beyond'; *Collected Poems*, p. 53)

When the reader has overcome his surprise at discovering that 'stillicide' is not a crime, he may notice how the 'still' reinforces the implications of whispering, muted and lone. If Hardy *was* forced by rhyme to employ the word, he certainly made full use of its faint connotations as well as its denotative accuracy.

6

A poet's coinages are nearly always interesting since we want to know, if possible, why the existing language did not supply his requirements, particularly when he has shown himself willing to select from the whole range of the language, standard and dialectal. There are 232 words listed under 'coined' in Dr Hickson's list (which does not include *The Dynasts* or *The Queen of Cornwall*). It is difficult to make a representative choice, since they are a very mixed class. A considerable proportion are affix-constructions of the type discussed earlier; for example 'foreframed', 'outcreep', 'thence-wise', 'unfulfil', 'updated', and so on. There are words of surprising simplicity such as 'dismantlers' and 'hearthside', and economical compounds such as 'housebacks', 'branch-ways' and 'graveacre'. Dr Hickson's lists are useful as indications, but there are errors in them, besides omissions and dubious classifications; thus 'homealong' is not invented, but Dorset dialect; Hardy's part in the creation of 'graveside' seems limited to the omission of a hyphen, and he certainly did not invent 'shawm'.

In fact, most of Hardy's coinages are improvements in concision and metrical convenience. As such they are, *normally*, evidence not of Hardy's concern with meaning, but of the technical care he exercised, despite continual accusations of clumsiness. An example is to be found in the last line of 'The Change':

> The heart whose sweet *reverberances* are all time leaves
> to me.   (*Collected Poems*, p. 427)

'Reverberances' is apparently Hardy's own invention to avoid the metrical awkwardness of 'reverberations' (used by him in 'A Singer Asleep'). The coinage is a fairly obvious one and unimportant on the level of meaning. His willingness to use all the resources of the language is such that although, as we have seen, minor variations and combinations which produce technically new words are relatively common, real innovations are rare.

Five words have been selected as examples of differing kinds of innovation and variation: 'vespering' ('The Year's Awakening'); 'aftergrinds' ('Honeymoon Time at the Inn'); 'dampered' ('Haunting Fingers'); 'freshlings' ('A House with a History'); and 'fantocine' ('He Wonders about Himself').

> O *vespering* bird, how do you know,
> How do you know?
>
> (*Collected Poems*, p. 315)

'Vespering', probably derived immediately from 'vesper', is connected with 'vespertine' which has the 'zoological sense of appearing or flying in the early evening'. In addition to this preciseness and the implication of singing in the evening, the connotations of the word (declining sun and light) are felt in the poem, which is based on the anomaly that signs of reviving life are seen at a time of year when life seems to be at a very low ebb. (The use of 'belting' in the same poem is another example of Hardy's slightly grotesque accuracy.)

> 'It's good,' said the Spirits Ironic, 'to tickle their minds
> With a portent of their wedlock's *aftergrinds*.'
>
> (*Collected Poems*, p. 485)

Here what was even in Hardy's day mainly a slang usage (grind = unpleasant toil) is combined with one of his favourite prefixes to create an effective coinage.

> '—I rejoiced thereat!'
> (Thuswise a harpsicord, as 'twere from *dampered* lips.)
>
> (*Collected Poems*, p. 559)

There are two archaic words ('thereat' and 'thuswise') and one invention, in a concentrated example of the mélange which Hardy can make into his own idiom. 'Dampered' is derived from 'damper' (a pad silencing the strings of a piano), which is first transformed into a past participle and then attributed to the harpsichord's 'lips' to indicate the low, suppressed tone. Again the connotations are effective.

> And who are peopling its parlours now?
>   Who talk across its floor?
> Mere *freshlings* are they, blank of brow,
>   Who read not how
> Its prime had passed before.

>   (*Collected Poems*, p. 609)

'Freshling' is an example of a coinage adopted for precision which is almost, if not quite, something more than merely precise; the linking of a common adjective with a common diminutive seems obvious and simple—once it has been done.

> No use hoping, or feeling vext,
> Tugged by a force above or under
> Like some *fantocine*, much I wonder
> What I shall find me doing next!

>   (*Collected Poems*, p. 479)

'Fantocine' is derived from the Italian 'fantoccini', puppets. It is accurate enough, though puppet would be too. What would be lost if puppet were used would be the alliterating 'f', one per line and each on a heavily stressed syllable. The unfamiliar, slightly mysterious word emphasizes too, I think, the mysterious situation of the speaker and the unknown mysterious forces which are acting on him.

7

Discussions of rare words and peculiar usages, contorted syntax and linguistic mixtures, always occupy a large part of any discussion of Hardy's language. This is natural enough, but probably unfortunate in the long run. In the first place there is a natural tendency to exaggerate their frequency and their strangeness. (Less than 1 per cent of Browning's 34,746 rhymes are either imperfect or forced, but these have been enough to give him a reputation for eccentric rhyming.)[1] In the second (if one must look for Hardy's weaknesses), it distracts attention from the area of true weakness. The really unsatisfactory work is not the odd, strained, gnarled, 'mixed' poems, but those whose technical accomplishment covers hollowness. Such poems as 'A Bygone Occasion', 'The Rift', 'I Look in Her Face', 'Could I but Will' and 'I Knew a Lady' are quite vacuous, unless one considers that it is interesting to know that Hardy was influenced by the Victorian drawing-room ballad. Poems such as 'The Two Wives' and 'The Singing Woman' are in their different ways products of the desire to write poems which, as we saw in an earlier chapter, is part of Hardy's poetical physiology. All these are linguistically smooth and all are ultimately worthless.

The badness of 'My Cicely', pointed out by several critics, is a special kind of badness—Hardy's. The poem, therefore, has its own attractions, since Hardy's good work as well as his bad depends on—or is an extension of—his personality. (McDowall, perceptive as usual, calls it 'a curious and shadow-haunted poem'.)[2] Critics never seem to object to 'Any Little Old Song'; it has appeared in several anthologies and selections (including the Penguin *Hardy* in 1960), but it seems to me to be completely negligible, from its ominous title onwards. The linguistic deadness of this poem is clear enough. It is, however, easy to jump to unwarranted conclusions about Hardy's use of similar language. Mrs

[1] H. H. Hatcher, *The Versification of Robert Browning* (Columbus, Ohio, 1928), p. 108.
[2] McDowall, p. 245.

Nowottny gives a general account of this problem: 'the diffi-
culty for the critic, especially when there is no conspicuous
innovation at the level of vocabulary, is to arrive at an
understanding of those processes in the poem which enable
familiar words to convey unique quality' (p. 105).

It is fairly easy to find places where this difficulty has been
too much for the critic, or has never been faced at all; for
instance:

> They [Hardy's poems] have their share of stuffed-owl sim-
> plicities, such as the observation in the railway waiting room,
>> The table bore a Testament
>> For travellers' reading, if suchwise bent.
>
> (Blunden, p. 264)

We can only agree—if this gobbet is accepted as the solitary
piece of evidence for the charge; but this is a stultifying
procedure. If one reads 'In a Waiting Room' instead, one
finds that it begins in this way:

> On a morning sick as the day of doom
>> With the drizzling gray
>> Of an English May,
> There were few in the railway waiting-room.
> About its walls were framed and varnished
> Pictures of liners, fly-blown, tarnished.
> The table bore a Testament
> For travellers' reading, if suchwise bent.
>
> (*Collected Poems*, p. 487)

Surely the drabness of the last phrase is in key with every-
thing else? Is not the scene, the situation and the feeling well
rendered? Furthermore, is the phrase so drab really? Is
there not a subdued irony to it—an implication that nobody
will be so bent? This is heightened when we find that the

plainest evidence of its having been used is that some
commercial traveller ('bagman' is Hardy's word) has been
doing his calculations on the Gospel of St John!

Another example:

Much might be said of these few stanzas only ['In Tenebris I'].
I will only note: the simplicity of their metrical structure, the
perfect carrying-through of the stated theme: contrasted with
this, the awkwardness in places of the diction, the obstinate
choice—as it seems, for careless it is not—of the lifeless word

No more that severing scene
Can *harrow* me . . .   (Young, p. xxvi)

This is plainly a more subtle misunderstanding. Young has
specifically excluded carelessness and seems to be considering
the word in context; but is 'harrow' lifeless and, if not, why
does he fall foul of it?

The first thing to notice is that the poem is not only about
despair and 'unhope' but the pain connected with them;
'pain', 'smart', 'scath', 'faint'; next to remember what a
harrow does to the ground; then to observe 'severing' in the
previous line. 'Harrow' is part of a powerful image cluster,
not a lifeless word. We ought to notice, too, the heavy
stress on the word; it is not intended to be passed over
lightly in any sense.

The short answer to the second question is that Young,
typical here of many critics, thought it lifeless because his
preconceived ideas about Hardy caused him to expect lifeless
diction:

He was imperfectly educated, cramped by a book-language
which he could not shake himself free of, and writing it with a
stilted and self-conscious clumsiness. . . .

His errors are not those of an untrained taste feeling towards a style which will not come. They are errors of practice in following unfortunate models—prose translations of the classics, for example—without perceiving their imperfection. p. xiv)

The danger inherent in this attitude is that when an author gets a reputation for clumsiness the quality of his words may no longer be noticed at all.

8

I emphasized earlier that most of Hardy's triumphs are poems which subdue difficulties *and* show signs of the struggle; smoothness and ease are frequently danger signals. It would be strange if this were always so; he does have his less idiosyncratic successes, as 'I Look into My Glass':

> I look into my glass,
> And view my wasting skin,
> And say, 'Would God it came to pass
> My heart had shrunk as thin!'
>
> For then, I, undistrest
> By hearts grown cold to me,
> Could lonely wait my endless rest
> With equanimity.
>
> But Time, to make me grieve,
> Part steals, lets part abide;
> And shakes this fragile frame at eve
> With throbbings of noontide.

(*Collected Poems*, p. 72)

The linguistic variation here is no greater than is to be expected among good poems; it is, in fact, one of the few successful Hardy poems which could be by someone else.

(There is a resemblance to Yeats, whose Song, 'I thought no more was needed', might almost be an answer to it, since it takes the opposite side in the Body/Soul conflict.)

On the other hand, 'The Pedigree' would be spotted instantly as Hardy; situation, structure, theme, are all typical. The surprising thing is that the vocabulary is much less so; a 'Hardy' effect has been obtained with a standard, consistent, vocabulary. Only when this has been achieved do the usual peculiarities appear.

> I bent in the deep of the night
> Over a pedigree the chronicler gave
> As mine; and as I bent there, half-unrobed,
> The uncurtained panes of my window-square let in the watery light
> Of the moon in its old age:
> And green-rheumed clouds were hurrying past where mute and cold it globed
> Like a drifting dolphin's eye seen through a lapping wave.
>
> (*Collected Poems*, p. 431)

In 'At Castle Boterel' we see something different again; this is a poem mainly in a very plain style, but at one point it modulates into 'Hardy' language and out again without incongruity. First come five stanzas of what might be described as impressive ordinariness; then

> And to me, though Time's unflinching rigour,
>   In mindless rote, has ruled from sight
> The substance now, one phantom figure
>   Remains on the slope, as when that night
>   Saw us alight.
>
> I look and see it there, shrinking, shrinking,
>   I look back at it amid the rain

M

For the very last time; for my sand is sinking,
And I shall traverse old love's domain
Never again.

(Collected Poems, p. 331)

'Time's unflinching rigour' and 'mindless rote' are typical
examples of his philosophical language; 'phantom' is a
favourite word; 'ruled' shows a boldness of metaphor not in
evidence elsewhere in the poem. But they arise naturally out
of the precise situation and provide a slight generalization in a
very individual poem; which then returns to its concrete
situation and language. The two changes of linguistic level are
achieved smoothly and the sixth stanza is not at odds with
the others.

To show how Hardy's use of language enables his poems
to live 'on the dangerous edge of things', as so many of
them do, it is necessary to consider a complete poem.

The Five Students

The sparrow dips in his wheel-rut bath,
The sun grows passionate-eyed,
And boils the dew to smoke by the paddock-path;
As strenuously we stride,—
Five of us; dark He, fair He, dark She, fair She, I,
All beating by.

The air is shaken, the high-road hot,
Shadowless swoons the day,
The greens are sobered and cattle at rest: but not
We on our urgent way,—
Four of us; fair She, dark She, fair He, I, are there,
But one—elsewhere.

Autumn moulds the hard fruit mellow,
And forward still we press

Through moors, briar-meshed plantations, clay-pits yellow,
As in the spring hours—yes,
Three of us; fair He, fair She, I, as heretofore,
But—fallen one more.

The leaf drops: earthworms draw it in
At night-time noiselessly,
The fingers of birch and beech are skeleton-thin
And yet on the beat are we,—
Two of us; fair She, I. But no more left to go
The track we know.

Icicles tag the church-aisle leads,
The flag-rope gibbers hoarse,
The home-bound foot-folk wrap their snow-flaked heads,
Yet I still stalk the course—
One of us . . . Dark and fair He, dark and fair She, gone:
The rest—anon.

(*Collected Poems*, pp. 463-4)

The first task, undertaken mainly through language, is the
neutralizing of possibly ludicrous associations, since memor-
ies of 'Ten Little Nigger Boys' can be aroused by the poem.
This is done mainly by the almost complete cutting out of
details regarding the fates of the students; there is only the
laconic 'elsewhere' or 'fallen one more'. This avoids the
mistake Wordsworth made in 'We are Seven':

The first that died was sister Jane:
In bed she moaning lay,
Till God released her of her pain;
And then she went away.

The next trouble is that of Stock Responses; there are two
possible, based on the Seasons/Life parallel and the 'I am

left alone by death of friends' motif. It must be admitted that the poem does depend, to some extent, upon these responses, but they are controlled by a precise use of words; the effect is worked for, and there is no encouragement to the reader to construct his own poem. This is achieved (in contrast to the deaths) by a delicate use of detail. The 'mechanical' nature of the poem's progression is lessened by slight variations; for instance, the changes in the order of the students in line 5.

The key to the first stanza is violence: 'dips', 'wheel-rut', 'passionate-eyed', 'boils', 'strenuously', 'beating'. Thus, one of the stock associations of Spring is used, but the other, delicacy (young tender leaves and so forth), is contradicted. The sparrow, it should be noted, is not a 'romantic' bird. The second, Summer, stanza has for its key, still heat ('hot', 'shadowless', 'swoons', 'sobered', 'rest'). 'Sobered' was originally 'darkened' and it is one of Hardy's good revisions; it is not only exact but provides a link by contrast to the first stanza; 'shaken' sounds violent, but probably refers to heat-haze, not thunder. In the third, Autumn, stanza, the 'hurrying' word is 'press', which is milder than the 'strenuously' of the first stanza and the 'urgent' of the second; the implication of 'briar-meshed' points the same way. The semantic connection between 'mould' and 'press' probably plays its part too.

The fourth stanza, early Winter, is full of quietness, stillness and menace ('drop', 'earthworms', 'noiselessly', skeleton-thin', 'fingers'). The earthworm image could have been imitated from Tennyson's 'Geraint and Enid',

> While some, whose souls the old serpent long had drawn
> Down, as the worm draws in the wither'd leaf
> And makes it earth . . .

since both are rather menacing. But the idea is hardly out of the way.

The last stanza, dead of Winter, depends of course upon cold. The visual accuracy of the first line and the aural of the second are both important. There is, I think, a ghostly effect created from 'gibber', via the 'squeak and gibber' of the Roman ghosts mentioned in *Hamlet*. (This may be far-fetched, but the connection was made by me and another reader independently).

Words which have to be considered are 'beating', 'beat' and 'stalk' (which was objected to in 'In Time of the "Breaking of Nations" '). The primary meaning is 'to march proudly' which is accurate here. The O.E.D. adds that it is frequently used of ghosts, plagues, etc., which tends to support the possible implications of 'gibber'. The meaning is different from that of 'stalk' in 'In Time of the "Breaking of Nations" ' so Hardy is evidently in full control of this word. With regard to 'beat', 'a course habitually traversed by anyone', the chief points are to note the word 'habitually', and to be unaffected by the modern limitation of the word to police-men. 'Beating' is presumably 'beating a path', though intransitive uses in this sense are rare.

There are a number of compounds in the poem; 'wheel-rut', 'paddock-path', 'briar-meshed', etc. One line has three:

The home-bound foot-folk wrap their snow-flaked heads.

Frequent use of compounds is one of the marks of Hardy's style, as mentioned earlier. Often they are alliterative, e.g. 'paddock-path', 'foot-folk', and Dr Hickson has a long list of these. (The use of such linked nouns as 'ball and blade', 'sun and shower' is common also, especially in Hardy's poorer poems; for instance, 'And kings invoked for rape

and raid/His fearsome aid in rune and rhyme', 'The Sick
Battle-God', *Collected Poems*, pp. 88–9.) Groom points
out that some of the examples of compounds he gives
(e.g. 'copse-cloth'd', 'coppice-crowned') 'have a certain
piquancy and in their context are suggestive of pathos; but
of the delicate touch which changes the ordinary into the
poetic, they show not a trace' (see p. 145). This is perhaps
overstated, but it is hard to disagree with his opinion that
Hardy uses them mainly for compression or as 'a useful
metrical expedient'.

Here, as often, one must distinguish between use and
origin. Dorset dialect—much closer to Anglo-Saxon—
undoubtedly could provide a sense of familiarity with
compounds: 'if you ask one of the workfolk (they always
used to be called "workfolk" hereabout—"labourers" is
an imported word') (*Later Years*, p. 94). 'Foot-folk' is ob-
viously normal enough to anyone with such a background.
The frequent use of compounds is, perhaps, one reason for
the high proportion of monosyllables in the poem (noted
by Evelyn Hardy, p. 134). Finally, on page 201 of Purdy's
Thomas Hardy: A Bibliographical Study the reader can see
two unpublished stanzas of this poem. They prove that if
Hardy often wrote inferior verse he did not always publish it.

Accusations of a monotonous obsession with Death lose
much of their sting—and truth—when we see how different
in tone Hardy's handlings of the subject are. His elegy on
his mother is a striking variation on the theme.

After the Last Breath
(J.H. 1813–1904)

There's no more to be done, or feared, or hoped;
None now need watch, speak low, and list, and tire;

No irksome crease outsmoothed, no pillow sloped
        Does she require.

Blankly we gaze. We are free to go or stay;
Our morrow's anxious plans have missed their aim;
Whether we leave tonight or wait till day
        Counts as the same.

The lettered vessels of medicaments
Seem asking wherefore we have set them here;
Each palliative its silly face presents
        As useless gear.

And yet we feel that something savours well;
We note a numb relief withheld before;
Our well-beloved is a prisoner in the cell
        Of Time no more.

We see by littles now the deft achievement
Whereby she has escaped the Wrongers all,
In view of which our momentary bereavement
        Outshapes but small.

(Collected Poems, pp. 253–4)

This elegy is not one of Hardy's pondering poems. The tone, firm but not dogmatic, is that of a man quietly confident that he knows what he thinks and what he is going to say. The form, perhaps based on the Sapphic stanza of Hardy's favourite Latin poet, Horace, is well adapted to this form of speech; the three long lines, slow-moving but free from contortion, are succeeded by the 'clinching' short line which rounds off each stanza, marking firmly each stage in the argument. Hardy frequently ends a poem with a slight variation in the structure and here the final double rhyme provides one.

When considered linguistically, the poem shows a similar

care and tone. The first stanza has at the beginning an unbroken run of monosyllables; the change comes with 'no irksome crease outsmoothed', itself an effective mixture since the harshness of 'irksome' is followed logically by the softness of 'outsmoothed', paralleling the action itself. The quiet felicity of 'sloped' is notable, but easy to miss.

Stanza 2 is again largely monosyllabic. The key word both in sound and meaning is 'anxious', emphasizing the uncertainty of the mourners as to whether they would be able to carry out their provisional intentions. The heavily polysyllabic opening of stanza 3 contrasts with most of the poem so far, and the contrast is heightened in the third line where the Latinate 'palliative' stands against the flat colloquialism of 'silly face'.

Stanza 4 is, by comparison, a little romantic; for instance. 'savours', 'well-beloved', 'prisoner in the cell of Time', The fine paradox is striking, however. The final stanza begins with the bold telescoping of 'little by little' to 'littles', followed by the syllabic contrast of 'deft achievement' and two typical Hardyan usages, the personification of 'Wrongers' and the affix-contruction 'outshapes'. Finally, 'momentary bereavement' turns this elegy for one person into a *memento mori* for himself and us; the bereavement is but momentary since everyone's time is short.

9

Another favourite subject for discussion is words which may not be themselves outstanding or peculiar, but are characteristic of Hardy and his verse. One group, despite the attention it has attracted, is ultimately of little importance; this is composed of the words which embody Hardy's philosophical presumptions; 'rote-restricted', 'Doomsters', 'Willer', 'Automaton', and so on. They are not very common outside *The Dynasts* and objections to them usually turn out to be objections to the philosophy itself. To defend them is easy; to be enthusiastic about them is admittedly rather more difficult.

A second, and probably more important, group consists of very ordinary words which Hardy used frequently and seemed to attach special value to. Hynes has commented unfavourably upon these and it is true that Hardy's habits here seem to be in contradiction with those previously observed. Hynes points out that 'phantom', though commonly meaning an actual spirit from the dead, carries other meanings; impermanence, unreality, imagination and memory. He admits that the dictionary will support most of these meanings, but maintains that usually the word 'has lost its sharp distinctions of meaning, and has become simply a word for a vague emotion' (p. 96). He deals in a similar manner with 'pale', remarking that 'By calling a thing "pale" he assigned an emotion to it, and we must simply accept the assertion that the emotion is really there if we are to respond adequately to the poem' (p. 98); and with 'rare': 'The word, like other favourite words, must be taken on faith, as meaning what Hardy says it means' (p. 99).

I find myself in agreement with a great deal here, as I often do with Dr Hynes, especially as he shows himself to be aware that these words and this kind of usage do not exist in isolation. Hardy seems to be trying to use these words as a kind of emotional tuning-fork to put the reader on the right note and this does lead to a certain haziness about precise meaning. Hynes uses as his chief example of 'phantom', 'The Lament of the Looking-Glass'.

> I flash back phantoms of the night
> That sometimes flit by me,
> I echo roses red and white—
> The loveliest blooms that be—
> But now I never hold to sight
> So sweet a flower as she.
>
> (*Collected Poems*, p. 638)

He comments:

> The significance of *phantoms* in this stanza is at best imprecise. It stands in the catalogue of corporeal things which are not worth reflecting now that 'she' is dead; but in this catalogue *phantoms* has no necessary role—its presence suggests an automatic response to a need for something mysterious, rather than conscious selection. (p. 96)

My feeling of agreement with this is strengthened by the presence of 'flash' in the same line. This is another word which Hardy sometimes used as a maid of all work. The following examples are to be found within a stretch of only six poems, the last three within four poems:

> A messenger's knock cracks smartly,
> Flashed news is in her hand.
>
> ('A Wife in London')

> His crimson form, with clang and chime,
> Flashed on each murk and murderous meeting-time.
>
> ('The Sick Battle-God')

> When from Torino's track I saw thy face first flash on me
>
> ('Genoa and the Mediterranean')

> Whom common simples cure, her act flashed home.
>
> ('In the Old Theatre, Fiesole')

But even when faced with this kind of thing in addition to Hynes's observations, it is necessary to be cautious and fair. It is easy to get the impression that the use of 'phantom', for example, is *always* loose; a glance at 'At Castle Boterel' will show that this is not so. Examination of Hynes's examples of the use of 'pale' shows him to be largely overlooking the fact that 'pale' has common connotations of weakness, faintness and general lack of vigour. This is particularly marked in the example he gives from 'Night in the Old Home'; 'A pale late plant of your once strong stock?' (Hardy himself). One needs to know only a little of Hardy's family history and his view of it to realize that the word carries enough precision for a sympathetic reader.

It is possible, however, to consider this matter in a rather wider context; Dr Hynes comes close to doing so when he connects Hardy's use of 'phantom' with his half-belief in 'spectres, mysterious voices, intuitions, omens, dreams, haunted places, etc.' (*Later Years*, p. 271), and what Hynes calls 'his fondness for the trope of the ghostly visitant' (p. 97) ('pale' carries similar implications frequently). This takes a step in the right direction, since it connects the diction with the thoughts and emotions of Hardy himself; these words are part of Hardy's personal idiom, a necessary consequence of his need for expression, particularly for expression of emotion, and as M. H. Abrams has remarked: 'In any theory that poetry is an expression of feeling, the question of diction tends to become primary'.[1]

Hynes claims, correctly, that many of these words have to be taken on trust. That Hardy frequently fails to enable his readers to do more than this is clear enough; it would probably have needed a great and self-critical talent to do

[1] M. H. Abrams, *The Mirror and the Lamp* (New York, 1953), p. 110.

so. What Hardy wanted was something which it has taken the combined work of many poets to achieve with other words and images.

Evocativeness is the power of an image to evoke from us a response to the poetic passion. An image need not be novel in order to do this; there are well-worn words such as moon, rose, hills, West—'Consecrated images', Mr G. W. H. Rylands calls them—which always tend to create this response.[1]

Hardy, in fact, seems to be attempting the rather desperate feat of trying to create a kind of private, consecrated imagery. The fact of ultimate failure should not distract us from appreciating the motive for the attempt. It was *his* vision which he wanted to express, which he would have found impossible if he had tried to use someone else's consecrated imagery.

The following example has, I think, interest because we can see Hardy using two linguistic modes at the same time:

> In the towns I am tracked by phantoms having weird
> detective ways—
>
> ('Wessex Heights'; *Collected Poems*, p. 300)

If the whole of 'Wessex Heights' is considered, as it plainly should be, then the felicity of 'detective' is obvious; the speaker is being dogged by mysterious, unfriendly beings. 'Ways', however, is qualified by a second adjective, 'weird', and the value of this is less obvious. One expects phantoms to have weird ways; one of the recognized meanings is, 'appertaining to phantoms or spirits'. It cannot be said, therefore, that anyone who believes the word to be redundant is necessarily wrong. If one really responds to Hardy, however (and it is possible to appreciate some of his

[1] C. Day Lewis, *The Poetic Image* (London, 1947), p. 40.

poetry, at least, without doing so), one understands that to him ghosts are more or less normal. He refers to himself as a kind of ghost while still alive (*Early Life,* p. 275); as half believing in supernatural phenomena of all kinds (*Later Years,* p. 168); to seeing people as automatons (*Early Life,* p. 241); to regarding inanimate objects as saturated with the thoughts and glances of others (*Later Years,* p. 17). Such poems as 'He Revisits His First School' should be read with these tendencies kept in mind.[1] The striking thing about the phantoms of 'Wessex Heights' is that their ways are *not* normal—they are active, hostile, dogging, or, to use his own word, 'weird'.

10

Despite the serious objections which have been made against Hardy's verbal amalgam, much of his strength is derived from it. If some of his words are rare, they are often fitting as well; if they are dialect, they remind us of what standard English has lost; if archaic, they frequently justify their revival; and if invented, they are sometimes worth the trouble. Hardy's own needs take precedence over the rules of others. This mélange, which does not seem a possible language for any human being, has been made into a personal, living, language. Hardy has created it to enable

---

[1] Florence Hardy in a letter dated 27 Dec. 1919 (p. 305 of Meynell's *Friends of a Lifetime*) tells of an encounter Hardy had with a ghost; the striking thing is his stolidity when confronted with this visitant. Presumably his attitude was the same as that recounted in 'The Woman I met'

> . . . That a phantom should stalk there
> With me seemed nothing strange, and talk there
> That winter night
> By flaming jets of light.

(*Collected Poems* p. 562)

him to say certain things. He is at the farthest extreme from
'... the perfect type of English secondary writer, con-
demned recently but for all time by Henri Davray with his:
"Ils cherchent des sentiments pour les accommoder à leur
vocabulaire" '.[1] Rémy de Gourmont has provided an even
more apposite summary: 'Le style est une spécialisation de la
sensibilité.'

The places where this personal idiom emerges most
clearly are such poems as 'To an Unborn Pauper Child',
'Nature's Questioning' and 'A Commonplace Day'. It is
significant that these poems have already been quoted as
examples of excellence in some other category; significant
not necessarily of a small number of good poems, but of the
way in which the poems are integrated; achievement in one
mode accompanies achievement in another. Another poem
which shows how an apparently disparate vocabulary has
been forced into a personal style is 'In Front of the Land-
scape'.

Plunging and labouring on in a tide of visions,
  Dolorous and drear,
Forward I pushed my way as amid waste waters
  Stretching around,
Through whose eddies there glimmered the customed landscape
  Yonder and near

Blotted to feeble mist. And the coomb and the upland
  Coppice-crowned,
Ancient chalk-pit, milestone, rills in the grass-flat
  Stroked by the light,
Seemed but a ghost-like gauze, and no substantial
  Meadow or mound.
        (*Collected Poems*, p. 285)

[1] Ezra Pound, *A B C of Reading* (London, 1934), p. 88.

There is obviously much to comment upon here besides the vocabulary. The stresses are strong and yet the rhythm seems fluid and supple enough. There is a rhyming-link, sustained through the poem, by which the fourth line in the first stanza of a pair supplies the rhyme for the second and sixth lines of the second stanza. To attack the vocabulary is only too easy; 'Dolorous and drear' seems too vague to mean anything. It is used in a (probably) early poem 'The Lost Pyx', and 'drear' is one of Hardy's early vogue words; even he seemed to realize his weakness since two of its four uses in *Wessex Poems* were removed by revision; there is the peculiar 'customed' and the 'dead' compound 'ghost-like'. But the description, despite its occasional verbal precision, e.g. 'rills in the grass-flat/Stroked by the light' and conciseness, e.g. 'coppice-crowned', is intended to be ominous and generally vague; the idea of moving through a 'tide of visions' would be ludicrous if allowed to become too vivid; 'customed' landmarks are indistinct and unsubstantial. This welding of manner and matter continues throughout: for example, the last two stanzas:

Thus do they now show hourly before the intenser
            Stare of the mind
As they were ghosts avenging their slights by my bypast
            Body-borne eyes,
Show, too, with fuller translation than rested upon them
            As living kind.

Hence wag the tongues of the passing people, saying
            In their surmise,
'Ah—whose is this dull form that perambulates, seeing nought
            Round him that looms
Whithersoever his footsteps turn in his farings,
            Save a few tombs?'   (*Collected Poems*, p. 287)

Among other things, there should be noted the precise successful use of 'bypast'; the appropriateness of 'body-borne' (Hardy's alliterative compounds often justify themselves); the ambiguity of 'translation'; the colloquial 'wag'; the abstract 'surmise'; the learned 'perambulates'; the semi-archaic 'farings'; and the rightness here of another early vogue word 'looms' (four uses in *Wessex Poems* alone). All these should be noted; and also the way in which these recalcitrant words are yoked together, slaves to Hardy's meaning and intentions.

Mr Southworth observes rather grudgingly: 'Too persistent reading of his poetry dulls one's sense of incongruous or unfelicitous associations of strange bedfellows' (p. 126). Perhaps Hardy himself should be allowed to answer:

He subjoined the Dedication of *Sordello* where the author remarks: 'My faults of expression are many; but with care for a man or a book such should be surmounted, and without it what avails the faultlessness of either? (*Later Years*, p. 179)

VIII

Development

THE study of Hardy's poetic development is dominated by the fact that there is, compared with what we have for many poets, very little evidence. He was a late starter as a published poet and he did not normally keep working MSS, as distinct from fair copies. He sometimes dated poems, and there is no reason for doubting his reasonable accuracy; but most of the poems are not dated. The dates he does supply show that poems were retained in MS, sometimes for long periods, and this may be true of other, undated ones. It would be rash to assume that when a poem is undated publication always followed closely upon completion, or that there was no revision between the completion and publication of dated poems.

Before 1898, when Hardy was fifty-eight, objective information is very rare indeed, consisting of four published poems and one rough draft. Practically all other information comes directly or indirectly from remarks by Hardy himself. He was not in the habit of making inaccurate statements, but his omissions were many and important. Mrs Hardy's 'biography' omits a great deal and we are probably lucky to have as much information as we have. Deductions by the reader may attain a high degree of subjective certainty, but remain deductions.

Even the objective sources prove, besides being meagre, to be of little use. One poem, 'The Fire at Tranter Sweatley's'

N

(later 'The Bride-Night Fire'), is comic and completely in dialect. 'The Sergeant's Song' and 'The Stranger's Song' were published in prose works and were probably written for them. 'Lines' was an occasional piece and is in couplets (a rare form for Hardy). The rough draft, that of 'Retty's Phases', is interesting, but as it appears to be the sole MS survivor of a number of poems which Hardy describes as 'from an old note', no generalizations can be based upon it. Strictly speaking, therefore, we are reduced to considering the development of a poet from the age of nearly sixty onwards! In practice, I think that a great deal more can be assumed, provided that the difference between fact and probability is remembered.

About forty poems are dated as being written in the 1860s, the majority in the middle of the decade; 1866 is by far the most frequent date. Hardy tells us something about them.

. . . and by 1865 he had begun to write verses, and by 1866 to send his productions to magazines. That these were rejected by editors and that he paid such respect to their judgement as scarcely ever to send out a MS twice was in one feature fortunate for him, since in years long after he was able to examine those poems of which he had kept copies, and by the mere change of a few words or the rewriting of a line or two make them quite worthy of publication. (*Early Life*, p. 62)

A little later he says that he continued writing when the hope of immediate publication was gone (p. 64).

These poems are varied but some general tendencies can be observed. Probably the most immediately striking thing is the high proportion of sonnets, for example the 'She to Him' poems, 'In Vision I Roamed', 'Neutral Tones', 'Hap', 'A Confession to a Friend in Trouble', 'At a Bridal', 'Her Confession', 'To an Actress', 'Discouragement', 'Her Reproach'.

Some, for instance '1967' and 'Her Dilemma', seem to be based upon a sonnet-structure without achieving it. In fact the restless variation in form which is found later is lacking; the metres are largely iambic and the forms conventional.

Linguistically, it is hard to say much with any certainty in view of Hardy's remarks about revision (it seems likely that he would underestimate the changes rather than over-estimate them). One does notice, however, Hardy's idio-syncratic mixtures ('In Vision I Roamed' is a striking ex-ample); though the vocabulary which accompanies Hardy's 'philosophy' is almost entirely lacking; 'Hap' is the ex-ception. Another interesting thing is that Hardy has not achieved his own style; his utterance is partly muffled by other poet's styles—Shakespeare (as in the 'She to Him' Sonnets and 'Her Reproach'), with some traces of Swin-burne, and a great deal of nineteenth-century 'poetic diction'. There is a looseness and vagueness which, although never completely outgrown in the mature Hardy, is glaring in 'A Confession to A Friend in Trouble':

> Your troubles shrink not, though I feel them less
> Here, far away, than when I tarried near;
> I even smile old smiles—with listlessness—
> Yet smiles they are, not ghastly mockeries mere.

> A thought too strange to house within my brain
> Haunting its outer precincts I discern:
> —*That I will not show zeal again to learn*
> *Your griefs, and, sharing them, renew my pain.* . . .

> It goes, like murky bird or buccaneer
> That shapes its lawless figure on the main,
> And each new impulse tends to make outflee
> The unseemly instinct that had lodgement here;

> Yet, comrade old, can bitterer knowledge be
> Than that, though banned, such instinct was in me![1]

There is much here that is certainly Hardy, for good and bad; 'outflee', 'precincts', 'haunting', 'ghastly' ('ghast' and 'ghastly' seem to have been favourites of Hardy at this time, e.g. 'In Vision I Roamed' and 'Discouragement' whose last line

> And fosterer of visions ghast and grim
>
> (*Collected Poems*, p. 789)

is a kind of one-line anthology of early Hardy). There is more perhaps that is not; the matter seems to have been stretched out to fourteen iambic ten-syllabled lines; lines 9 and 10 are, at the same time, over-detailed and vague (compare the effective use of a similar image in 'Neutral Tones' which is, in fact, the next poem!). The materials for a genuine poem are here, but they have not coalesced into one. This is the outstanding defect of most of the early poems ('Hap' is again an exception). On page 204 of the *Collected Poems*, an interesting contrast can be seen. '1967' is clear, spare and precise, and this is so whether it makes one feel awe or want to giggle (I have heard both reactions reported). 'Her Definition' is a product of the mingling of Hardy and someone else, and is of interest mainly on account of this.

It is on subject, however, that the critic's attention is likely to be concentrated finally. Practically all the Hardyan themes and obsessions of later years are there, but the proportions are rather different. (Here it is necessary to remind ourselves that we are forced to deal only with what has

[1] *Wessex Poems and Other Verses* (London, 1898), pp. 15–16. Cited as '1st Edit.'

survived, and without any guarantee that it has survived unaltered.) If we put aside the comic poems ('The Fire at Tranter Sweatley's' and 'The Ruined Maid'); the poems which are largely the result of Hardy's removal from rural Dorset to Metropolitan London ('From Her in the Country' and 'The Dream of the City Shopwoman'); the two poems addressed to an actress ('To an Impersonator of Rosalind' and 'To an Actress'); and, possibly, the poems which, although written in this decade, are later than the rest and draw their inspiration, it seems, from Hardy's residence at Weymouth in 1869 ('At Waking' and 'The Dawn after the Dance'), we have the core of Hardy's early work. It is personal, but not in the same way as many of the later poems are. Most of them could be classified as poems about Love or Reaction from it (e.g. 'Revulsion' and 'Neutral Tones'), but often they have fictional forms; for instance, the adoption of a female persona, which can be seen in the 'She to Him' poems, 'Her Definition', 'Her Reproach' and 'Her Confession'. ('Her Dilemma' was originally of this type. The MS shows 'I' instead of 'she' throughout.) These could have been based on unknown episodes in Hardy's life, but in their present forms they are inventions.

Some poems show rather strained attitudes (e.g. 'Revulsion', 'A Confession to a Friend'), which may be perhaps associated with Hardy's somewhat mysterious statement that he might 'do a volume of poems consisting of the *other side* of common emotions' (*Early Life*, p. 76). These 'core' poems are those which are in the derivative style discussed above; the combination of subject and style tends to make them distinctive. One can see traces of what is either an attempt to discuss the pro and contra of a subject or a tendency to versify opposing attitudes (e.g. 'From Her in the Country' and 'The Dream of a City Shopwoman'; 'Young Man's Epigram' and 'A Young Man's Exhortation'), which may well be an early form of Hardy's 'juxtaposition' habit. It is possible that the sonnet form is used so frequently because its characteristic ebb-and-flow employs a similar technique. Hardy's 'philosophy' is less prominent than it afterwards became, but can be seen in 'At a Bridal', 'Discouragement' and 'Hap' (the last is an exception to nearly every statement about Hardy's early work; the first seems to be one of the 'fictions' mentioned above).

It is a little surprising that the odd, quirky stories for which he is notorious are absent; unless one can regard some of the 'fictions' as modified versions of them. The two 'Weymouth' poems show a deepened note of sexual disillusion. If these are considered with a number of poems written later, but apparently drawing their inspiration from this period (for instance 'Her Father' and 'At a Seaside Town in 1869'), it appears that Hardy was concerned in, or witnessed, some events which he found disturbing.

The upshot of all this is, I think, that there is development in the poems, but to recognize it one must take everything into account; structure, vocabulary, ideas, tone and so on. What can be seen in the early poems are the characteristics of the later Hardy in weak solution; only occasionally (e.g. 'Hap' and 'Neutral Tones') has something occurred to precipitate them.

The next quarter century was unfruitful poetically. Hardy's statement, 'the middle period of his novel writing producing few or none' (*Later Years*, p. 66), is corroborated by the meagre harvest; about fifteen dated poems. Of these, 'Ditty' concerns Emma Hardy (the only one to do so during her lifetime, though 'The Minute before Meeting' possibly

refers to her too). 'He Abjures Love' seems a greatly im-
proved rehandling of the theme of 'Revulsion'.

In June 1868 Hardy 'recorded at some length the outline
of a narrative poem on the Battle of the Nile. It was never
finished, but it shows that the war with Napoleon was even
then in his mind as material for poetry of some sort' (*Early
Life*, p. 76). This and a later entry (*Early Life*, p. 140) belong
really to the history of *The Dynasts*. There are, however,
six handlings of Napoleonic themes in *Wessex Poems*; the
two dated were written or begun in 1878 and it is possible
that the others were. *The Trumpet Major* has a Napoleonic
background and, in fact, until Hardy stopped novel-writing,
the few poems he wrote often had close connection with the
novels.[1] Thus, 'In a Wood' (begun 1887) parallels *The
Woodlanders*, and Hardy's memories of Tryphena Sparks,
besides being part of the inspiration of *Jude the Obscure*,
resulted in two poems at least, 'Thoughts of Ph—a' and
'In a Eweleaze near Weatherbury'. Other poems which
may be connected with her are 'To an Orphan Child', 'Her
Immortality' and 'Her Death and After', all probably
written about this time. Now, however, Hardy was be-
ginning to produce poems in quantity again. The thin
trickle which had maintained the potentialities of the 1860s
widened and deepened and he became the prolific poet
which he remained for the rest of his life. It was during the
comparatively fallow period (fallow as far as verse was
concerned) between 1870 and 1890 that Hardy's style
formed or, perhaps better, concentrated itself. 'In A Wood',

[1] 'The Sergeant's Song' was first published in *The Trumpet Major* (1880)
and 'The Stranger's Song' in *The Three Wayfarers* (1883). One poem, 'She
to Him II', was 'prosed' in *Desperate Remedies*. (Wessex Edition, pp.
95–6).

'Thoughts of Ph—a', 'Ditty', 'He Abjures Love', 'The Minute before Meeting', 'After Reading Psalms XXXIX, XL, etc.' and the Napoleonic Ballads are 'Hardy'; some of the early poems were so, of course, but there were many exceptions.

From now onwards, what development there was can be studied best in fairly detailed vocabulary work. A general survey of themes is possible, but not, I think, very profitable; it is obvious enough that Hardy's philosophical poetry reached its height, in quantity at any rate, in the poems published in *Poems of the Past and the Present*, and that the death of Emma Hardy caused him to rise to a peak of both quantity and quality. Something can be said about the period of comparative decline and this will be done later.

I propose to examine the revisions of the text of *Wessex Poems*. A single volume has been chosen because otherwise a misleading result might be obtained by choosing 'interesting' revisions here and there; *Wessex Poems*, because, as this was Hardy's first volume of poetry, he had the longest time to amend it to what he wanted and it might be helpful to see what he thought needed alteration. Only *Wessex Poems* has been collated systematically, but a considerable proportion of the printed versions of the other volumes of poetry has been examined. The other major question which it is hoped to throw light on is that of Hardy's care about his poetry and concern for his text. Mr Robert Graves says, for instance, that Hardy told him 'that he was not interested in the fate of his poems once he had written them'.[1] An examination of successive editions might help to show how true this is.

---

[1] *The Crowning Privilege* (London, 1955), p. 20.

2

Wessex Poems, first published in 1898, consists of fifty-one poems, the composition of which covered over thirty years. Four had been previously published, two in prose works. After 1898, ten remained unchanged, except for the titles of three of them: 'Postponement', 'She', The Stranger's Song', 'The Ivy-Wife', 'Thoughts of Ph—a', 'Middle Age Enthusiasms', 'To An Orphan Child', 'At An Inn', 'The Slow Nature' and 'I Look into My Glass'.

A further ten underwent trifling alterations: 'Amabel', 'At a Bridal', 'Her Initials', 'Her Dilemma', 'She to Him IV', 'The Sergeant's Song', 'To Outer Nature', 'To a Lady', 'In a Eweleaze near Weatherbury', 'Heiress and Architect'. In 'The Sergeant's Song' a chorus line was re-written; otherwise, 'trifling' has been defined as the alteration of one word. The remaining thirty-one poems have been revised to a greater extent. This group of course shows considerable variation from one poem to another ('Lines', for instance, has little revision, 'My Cicely' a great deal).

The first significant matter which emerges concerns the poems which were revised. Although experience of critical disagreements makes one wary of making distinctions unless heavily qualified, I am strongly of the opinion that the poems of the third group, the revised group, are the best; which implies that when Hardy was, relatively, soon satisfied with a poem it was likely to be an inferior one.

If I had to reduce *Wessex Poems* to one quarter, and this is a higher proportion than most critics are willing to approve of, only two, 'Heiress and Architect' and 'I Look into My Glass' would be taken from the first two categories, compared with eleven from the third. There are thirty-one poems against twenty, and obviously the length of the poem is relevant, since the longer a poem, the more likely it is to be revised; but the disproportion is sufficiently marked as to make it unlikely to be the result of chance.

If the readings of the MS are taken into consideration, the tripartite distinction of No Revision, Slight Revision and Heavier Revision ceases to be formally significant, since only five poems, 'She', 'She to Him IV', 'The Sergeant's Song', 'To A Lady' and 'To an Orphan Child' were printed as they first appeared in the MS. In practice, however, the conclusion arrived at above is not essentially changed. Generally speaking, the poems which show least change in the MS show least revision later, and those with greater changes are those in which revision continued. Exceptions to this are too few to be of much consequence; 'Her Death and After' has few changes compared to the many subsequent ones, while on the other hand the MS of 'Thoughts of Ph—a', shows a considerable number of variants compared to its later stability; two poems, 'The Peasant's Confession' and 'The Dance at the Phoenix' have stanzas missing in MS (4 and 15 respectively) and 'The Impercipient' has an unpublished stanza after the third of the printed text. None of the omissions or additions seems important and the first two were heavily revised poems anyway. In one poem only, 'My Cicely', do we see the process of creation. After stanza 9 the MS reads as follows:

> By Egdon and Casterbridge [straightly] bore I
> Where legions had wayfared
> [I followed to mourn and entomb her]
> To tomb her I deemed sent to Silence
> [Whose star had darked He]
> By will of the Three.

Stanzas 10 and 11 of the first edition, and possibly 12 as well, have been developed from this.

Some of the variants will be considered in more detail later, but the conclusion concerning the connection between value and revision stands.

There are three points to consider; what the revisions were, when they were made and, if possible, why they were made.

The short answer to the second question appears to be, 'frequently'. Revision started with the second edition in 1903 and continued into the 1920s, when Hardy was over 80. To be more precise, revisions were made in 1903, 1911, 1912, 1916, 1919 and 1923. For instance, on page 36 of the *Collected Poems* is a line in 'Her Death and After', which in the first edition read:

> Scarce had night the sun's gold touch displaced

in the second edition of 1903:[1]

> Scarce night the sun's gold touch displaced

in the Wessex Edition 1912:[2]

> The sun's gold touch was just displaced

in the first Collected edition of the poems 1919:

> The sun's gold touch was scarce displaced.

It took four attempts and over twenty years for this not very important line to achieve its final form. The reasons for this persistent minor revision cannot be certainly known,

---

[1] *Wessex Poems and Other Verses* (London, 1903). Cited as '1903'.

[2] *Wessex Poems and Other Verses*; *Poems of the Past and the Present* (London, 1912) (The Wessex Edition). Cited as '1912'.

but even speculation may tell us something of Hardy's methods.

The first change, the omission of 'had', was probably metrical in origin. The second change put the verb into the passive, thus removing an inversion and arranging the line in a more natural order. The substitution of 'just' for 'scarce' removes a poeticism since current English would demand 'scarcely'. The final change, the reversion to 'scarce', was probably mainly in the interests of good English, since just = hardly is, or was, a vulgarism. As it returns to Hardy's first choice, however, there are possibly other reasons; for instance, 'just' carries an implication of exactness, a precise moment, which is undesirable in this context.

This enables us to give a preliminary answer to the third question; the possible reasons are numerous, e.g. better rhythm, better sentence-construction, more precise meaning. The answer to the first question, 'what were the revisions?', follows naturally and is what one would expect; they are improvements and clarifications of the original core or inspiration; not major modifications of it. One would expect this because Hardy's 'Wordsworthian' temperament made it the natural method of working for him; the experience is to be rendered more forcibly, but not essentially changed.

The only substantial addition to any of the Poems after publication is a stanza to 'San Sebastian' in 1912:

> Maybe we draw our children's guise
> From fancy, or one knows not what,
> And that no deep impression dies—
> For the mother of my child is not
> The mother of her eyes.

In 1919 the first two lines were revised to

> Maybe we shape our offspring's guise
> From fancy, or we know not what,

(the 1919 revision is the kind of slight improvement already noted). The interesting thing here is that, although the last two lines are probably the finest in the poem, the purpose of the stanza is obviously to eliminate a possible misunderstanding—that the daughter is the daughter of the Spanish girl; it is a clarification, not an alteration.

In one place only, I think, could it be held that a fundamental change has been made. The 1898 version of the end of 'A Meeting with Despair' was

> : Heaven's radiant show
> Had gone. Then chuckled he.

In 1912 this was amended to

> : Heaven's radiant show
> Had gone that heartened me.

This is an amendment of the familiar, standard, kind. The MS version, however, is

> : Heaven's radiant show
> Had gone: and gone had he.

It is possible to find more than one interpretation of this, but I think that the later versions merely bring out the implication which had been present from the start.

I believe that the connection between inspiration and revision can be seen elsewhere. As mentioned above, a number of poems in the book can probably be connected with Tryphena Sparks; 'Thoughts of Ph—a', 'In a Eweleaze near Weatherbury', 'To An Orphan Child', 'Her Death and After', 'Her Immortality'. The first three are renderings of fact, or actual feeling (the third was amended to 'To a

Motherless Child'; since Tryphena's daughter still had her father this change seems significant). It is not surprising to find that two show no revision after publication other than of title and one only trivial revision. The two remaining poems are rather different. 'Her Death and After' is plainly a piece of wishful thinking, an imaginary working-out of the situation depicted in 'To an Orphan Child'. This embodying of a real emotion in a fictitious situation is not the method which suits Hardy; a result is that this poem is the most heavily revised in *Wessex Poems* (apart, possibly, from 'The Fire at Tranter Sweatley's', a special case;[1] the runner-up is 'My Cicely', another poem about a dead, or 'pseudo-dead' love). The fifteenth stanza in the early editions ran as follows:

> One eve as I stood at my spot of thought
> In the white-stoned Garth, brooding thus her wrong,
> Her husband neared; and to shun his view
> By her hallowed mew
> I went from the tombs among.

In 1912 all except the first line was revised:

> In the white-stoned Garth with these brooding glooms,
> Her husband neared; and to shun his nod
> By her hallowed sod
> I went from among the tombs.

In the first collected edition of the Poems[2] Hardy reverted to the original text.

[1] This, Hardy's first published poem (in the Gentleman's Magazine, Nov. 1875), appeared in a very different form from later printings. It is clear, however, that both omissions and variations were the result of bowdlerizing. Later changes are almost entirely caused by heightening and then softening of the dialect.

[2] *Collected Poems of Thomas Hardy* (London, 1919). Cited hereafter as '1919'.

In 1923[1] he achieved a combination of the two:

> In the white-stoned Garth, brooding thus her wrong,
> Her husband neared; and to shun his nod
> > By her hallowed sod
> > I went from the tombs among.

These permutations could be explained on technical grounds, but it seems to me that they are partly due to Hardy's inability or unwillingness to be clear as to exactly what he meant; there was no 'truth' to relate and in fiction his vision tended to wobble.

'Her Immortality', whose theme connects it with this poem has the most frequently revised line in the book.

It wore ere life had sped	MS
It bore in maidenhead	1st Edit.
It bore ere breath had fled	1903
Of days ere she was wed	1912
reverts to 1903 reading	1919
It bore ere she was wed	1923

The tendency to combine two versions is noticeable here also—as is the uncertainty as to exactly what he means. (I find it significant that one of the most heavily revised poems in Hardy is 'The Supplanter' (*Collected Poems*, pp. 162–5); this is set in the same graveyard as 'Her Death and After' and is about a lost, betrayed, dead Love.)

3

The evidence so far has supported a *prima facie* case that Hardy's revisions were fairly frequent, rarely, if ever,

[1] *Collected Poems of Thomas Hardy* (2nd ed. London, 1923). Cited hereafter as '1923'.

affected theme, were intended to strengthen or clarify 'treatment', and sometimes revert to earlier versions, or modifications of them. Some attempt will now be made to give more widely-based evidence for these preliminary conclusions.

One can begin in a minor way by considering Hardy's dealings with the word 'and' in his revisions. It might seem that nothing of significance can be gathered from the use of such a common word, but I think that the cumulative evidence tells.

Then would I bear, and clench myself, and die,   1st Edit.
Then would I bear it, clench myself, and die   1912
                             ('Hap')

Her jewels, and least lace of personal wear;   1st Edit.
Her jewels, her least lace of personal wear;   1912
                   ('The Burghers')

Thereat he scowled on me, and pranced me near,
And pricked me with his sword.   1st Edit.
Thereat he scowled on me, and prancing near,   1912
He pricked me with his sword.
        ('The Peasant's Confession')

The mind from memory, and make Life all aim,   1st Edit.
The mind from memory, making Life all aim,   1912
               ('She to Him III')

She rose, and rayed, and decked her head   1st Edit.
She rose, arrayed, and decked her head   1912
          ('The Dance at the Phoenix')

And, as o'ernight, from Pummery Ridge   1st Edit.
As overnight, from Pummery Ridge   1912
          ('The Dance at the Phoenix')

And on them stirs, in lippings mere   1st Edit.
Upon them stirs, in lippings mere   1919
                    ('Nature's Questioning')

The prime reason for each of these amendments seems to be the desire for the removal of 'and', which is an outstanding example of words which are links but mean nothing in themselves; and Hardy's apparent dislike of such words has been mentioned earlier.

Although Hardy believed that there was value in *seeming* a little careless, there is no evidence that he thought awkward-ness as such was in any way valuable; and a number of revisions seem to originate in a desire to smooth or simplify the syntax of a sentence, e.g.

Fair Jenny's life had hardly been
    A life of modesty;
At Casterbridge experience keen
    Of many loves had she.   1st Edit.

Fair Jenny's life had hardly been
    A life of modesty;
And few in Casterbridge had seen
    More loves of sorts than she.[1]   1912
            ('The Dance at the Phoenix')

('Fair' was changed to 'Now' in 1919)

As though the master's ways
Through the long teaching days
Their first terrestial zest had chilled and overborne.   1st Edit.

As though the master's way
Through the long teaching day
Had cowed them till their early zest was overborne.   1912
                ('Nature's Questioning')

    [1] This is an exception, in that 'and' has been inserted.

o

('Way' and 'day' reverted to the original plural in 1919).

On the other hand, revisions sometimes show metrical considerations outweighing normal word order, e.g.

> Unto the place where I last saw   1st Edit.

> Unto the place where last I saw   1912
> ('Her Immortality')

In 'Her Death and After', there is a stanza where both factors seem to be operating simultaneously:

> A smarter grief within me wrought
> Than even at loss of her so dear;
> Dead the being whose soul my soul suffused,
> Her child ill-used,
> I helpless to interfere!   1st Edit.

> A smarter grief within me wrought
> Than even at loss of her so dear,
> That the being whose soul my soul suffused
> Had a child ill-used,
> I helpless to interfere!   1912

> A smarter grief within me wrought
> Than even at loss of her so dear
> That the being whose soul my soul suffused
> Had a child ill-used,
> While I dared not interfere!   1919

One of the reasons for revision was, as we have seen, clarification or sharpening of meaning. The last line of 'The Burghers' was altered to emphasize the point:

> —'Not mortal?' said he. 'Lingering—worse,' said I.   1st Edit.

> —'Mortal?' said he. 'Remorseful—worse,' said I.   1919

1923 reverts to the original reading.

The intention, if not the value of this change, is plain enough. In the first edition the first line of 'She to Him I' ran,

> When you shall see me lined by tool of Time

using the idea (common in Hardy) of Time as an abrading, boring, agent. In 1903, however, the line was changed to

> When you shall see me in the toils of Time.

The local improvement, if any, is very slight; but the change to a 'snaring' image undoubtedly fits better with the later reference to 'Sportsman Time'.

The last line of 'Her Initials' in the first edition read

> The radiance has died away.

In 1912 'died' was amended to 'waned'. Hardy evidently wanted the idea of gradual, natural, probably predestined disappearance; to get it, he was prepared to face the assonance of 'waned away'.

'Hard' was changed to 'long' in the eighth line of 'Her Dilemma' (1912) because the man has already been described as 'so wan and worn that he could scarcely stand'.

The ninth line of 'Revulsion' was changed from the original 'Let me then feel no more . . .' to 'Let me then never feel . . .' (1912), to sharpen the contrast upon which the poem is built. 'My Cicely' has several lines involved in such a change. The first edition read

> And by Weatherbury Castle, and therence
> Through Casterbridge, bore I,
> To tomb her whose light, in my deeming,
> Extinguished had He.

In 1903 'therence' was changed to 'thencefrom'. However, in 1911[1] the stanza was re-written:

[1] *Wessex Poems and Other Verses* (London, 1911). Cited as '1911'.

> And by Weatherbury Castle, and thencefrom
> Through Casterbridge held I
> Still on, to entomb her my vision
> Saw stretched pallidly.

Here the intention is to stress the persistence and stubbornness of the narrator, leading up naturally to his deliberate self-delusion. (In 1919 'vision' was changed to 'mindsight'.) One more example, out of several, shows this greater precision being achieved in stages. A line in 'The Dance at the Phoenix' read in the first edition

> To hide her ringlets thin;

In 1903, to emphasize Jenny's age by showing that she was grey as well, it read

> Where the bleached hairs ran thin.

In 1912 'ran' was altered to 'grew'—a further emphasis, I think, of Jenny's failing strength, which is soon to cause her death.

Although Hardy's vocabulary remained personal, the revisions to *Wessex Poems* show a lessening of these peculiarities. The following are a selection:

Love's race shows undecrease   1st Edit.

Love's race shows no decrease   1912
> ('Amabel')

> a creeping crush
Seemed inborne with the hours.   1st Edit.

> a creeping crush
Seemed borne in with the hours.   1912
> ('Leipzig')

| And, changing anew my onbearer | 1st Edit. |
| And, changing anew my blown bearer | 1912 |

('My Cicely')

| Who might have been, set on some outstep sphere, | 1st Edit. |
| Who might have been, set on some foreign Sphere, | 1912 |

('In Vision I Roamed')

| We'd stormed it at night, by the vlanker light | 1st Edit. |
| We'd stormed it at night, by the flapping light | 1912 |

('San Sebastian')

| O God, why this hocus satirific! | 1st Edit. |
| O God, why this seeming derision! | 1903 |

('My Cicely')

Even the rank poplars bear Illy a rival's air.	1st Edit.
Even the rank poplars bear Poorly a rival's air	*Selected Poems* (London, 1916)
Even the rank poplars bear Lothly a rival's air.	1919

('In a Wood')   (Errata slip)

| Iriséd embowment | 1st Edit. |
| Iris-hued embowment | 1912 |

('To Outer Nature)

(there are several examples of the use, and later removal, of an accented 'ed')

| And mirage mists their Shining Land Is a drear destiny | 1st Edit. |
| And mirage mists their Shining Land Is a strange destiny. | 1912 |

('The Impercipient')

(This is typical of the removal of several of Hardy's 'vogue' words: 'ghast' and 'drear'.)

The revisions show a tendency towards the removal of dialect and colloquial forms, and elisions. Examples of the former are given above and can be seen also in 'The Fire at Tranter Sweatley's'. Occasional examples of the latter are fairly common. A more concentrated patch can be seen in 'The Casterbridge Captains':

> That he had come, and they'd been stayed
> 'Twas but the chance of war:
> Another chance, and they'd sat here,
> And he had lain afar.
>
> Yet saw he something in the lives
> Of those who'd ceased to live ...   1st Edit.

In 1912 ' 'twas' changed to 'was' and in 1919 the other three contracted forms were removed.

It will be admitted that whatever may be thought of the revisions they show continuing care for the text, ranging from the whole poem to a single word. Many of the revisions are clearly improvements and most of the remainder are no worse. Retrogressions are rare, though, naturally, they exist. The revision of the original 'When, by mad passion goaded' ('Unknowing') into 'When panting passion-goaded' makes weakness worse. 'The Peasant's Confession' and 'The Alarm' show a number of revisions which change without improving.

4

It is quite possible to approve, individually, of nearly all Hardy's revisions and yet be doubtful about the general

tendency. The revisions show a slight, but persistent, move-
ment towards a style nearer that of standard English, and
I believe that much of the value of Hardy's poetry lies in the
idiosyncrasies which embody his personal vision. This is a
difficult matter to illustrate; so much depends on what one
reacts to in poetry in general and in some poet in particular;
the ambience of the poem, or even of a whole volume, is
relevant and yet impalpable. Nevertheless, the attempt has to
be made on a small scale; the place chosen is 'The Temporary
the All', particularly the first stanza. This poem was the first
in Hardy's first volume, which seems to indicate an intention
not to kow-tow to the public. The theme is typical Hardy,
the metre was not easy to grasp (in 1920 Hardy supplied
'Sapphics' as a sub-title), and the vocabulary very mixed
indeed. In short, the poem carries a strong tang of its writer.

> Change and chancefulness in my flowering youthtime,
> Set me sun by sun near to one unchosen;
> Wrought us fellowly, and despite divergence,
>   Friends interblent us.
>
> 'Cherish him can I while the true one forthcome—
> Come the rich fulfiller of my prevision;
> Life is roomy yet, and the odds unbounded.'
>   So self-communed I.
>
> Thwart my wistful way did a damsel saunter,
> Fair not fairest, good not best of her feather;
> 'Maiden meet,' held I, 'till arise my forefelt
>   Wonder of women.'
>
> Long a visioned hermitage deep desiring,
> Tenements uncouth I was fain to house in;
> 'Let such lodging be for a breath-while,' thought I
>   'Soon a more seemly.

'Then, high handiwork will I make my life-deed,
Truth and Light outshow; but the ripe time pending,
Intermissive aim at the thing sufficeth.'
　　Thus I . . . but lo, me!

Mistress, friend, place, aims to be bettered straightway,
Bettered not has Fate or my hand's achieving;
Sole the showance those of my onward earth-track—
　　Never transcended!

As early as 1903 the tenth line was revised,

　　　　Fair, the while unformed to be all-eclipsing;

and there was a further slight revision in 1912,

　　　　Fair, albeit unformed to be all-eclipsing;

In 1912 the end of the poem was altered; 'achieving' was
changed to 'achievement' and 'showance' to 'showings'—
two good examples of Hardy's tendency to smooth out his
verbal idiosyncrasies. The first stanza, however, is where his
revisory habits can be studied in some detail. The MS reads
as follows:

　　Change and chancefulness in my bloothing youthtime
　　Set me sun by sun near to one unchosen;
　　Wrought us fellowly, and despite misfortunes,
　　　　Friends interknit us.

It will be seen that two of the three revisions, 'misfortunes' to
'divergence' and 'interknit' to 'interblent', result in words of
stronger 'character', not weaker. The first two lines, once
published, remained unchanged, but in 1911 the remainder
read:

　　Wrought us fellow-like, and despite divergence,
　　　　Friends interlinked us.

The Wessex Edition of 1912 read:

    Wrought us fellowlike, and despite divergence
    Fused us in friendship.

It seems that Hardy had become uneasy about unusual words, the obsolete 'fellowly' and the rare 'interblent'. The next, more radical, revision reinforces the metal-working imagery ('wrought' and 'fuses') and tightens the syntax, since 'change and chancefulness' is now the subject of the whole sentence; the stanza is therefore more coherent, both in structure and imagery. The question is, how far these technical improvements are substantial improvements. The verbal oddities have for me an emotional penetrative power largely lacking in the final version, and the 'tidying up' seems of minor value when the poem as a whole remains much as it was. A real improvement would have meant a complete rewriting and therefore a different poem. There is another parallel here with Yeats, whose later style was undoubtedly superior to his earlier, but who sometimes spoiled the earlier poems by revisions in his later manner.

    Examination of the MS of *Wessex Poems* shows that the idiosyncrasies of diction which are part of Hardy's style are not caused by haste or carelessness. As mentioned earlier, many of them disappeared during revision and there is a temptation to assume that he was removing faults which he had overlooked, or roughness surviving from early drafts. The MS shows, on the contrary, that a change was much more likely to be in the direction of greater 'oddness' than in that of less; many of them came into the poem at a comparatively late stage, evidently because Hardy was not satisfied with the language of the poem as it stood. The following are selections:

I should have lived, uncaring all that lay   MS

I lived unware, uncaring all that lay 1st Edit.
    ('In Vision I Roamed')

If all such aimed ideals have such a close. MS

If the race all such sovereign types unknows. 1st Edit.
     ('At a Bridal')

And a few leaves lay on the withered sod. MS

And a few leaves lay on the starving sod. 1st Edit.
     ('Neutral Tones')

Such devilish din since war began MS

Such snocks and slats, since war began 1st Edit.
     ('Valenciennes')

. . . ; my milkwhite cow unslain; MS

. . . ; my capple cow unslain; 1st Edit.
    ('The Peasant's Confession')

I know the nod of night subdued, MS

I see the nightfall shades subtrude, 1st Edit.
    ('A Sign Seeker')

These changes should be compared with those on pages
200–1. There seems to be a kind of curve, as Hardy's taste for
the idiosyncratic increased and then diminished. The
quotations from 'Leipzig' show 'inborne' becoming 'borne
in', but the MS has 'narrowing', while in the quotation from
'San Sebastian', 'flapping', the 1912 revision, is in fact the
MS reading.

Many changes are improvements or clarifications of the
now familiar type. Changes which result in a lessening of
verbal idiosyncrasy, though fewer, are found. A striking one
occurs in 'Leipzig':

One road to the cincture, and but one,	MS
One road to the rearward, and but one	1st Edit.

It is tempting to say that his 'smoothing out' of vocabulary is the point at which Hardy's verse began to decline, but this is too simple. The process was largely completed by 1912, but his poetic height was reached between then and about 1920, the death of Emma Hardy obviously being the chief cause. What is true, I think, is that when this inspiration waned, the now established tendency to verbal smoothing showed up all the more clearly. The process was never irreversible; the language of the later poems is still idio-syncratic and sometimes revision makes it more so. For instance, in 'The Haunter' from *Satires of Circumstance*, 1914, p. 107 (*Collected Poems*, pp. 324–5), Hardy made three revisions which increased verbal idiosyncrasy:

> But cannot answer his words addressed me

becomes

> But cannot answer the words he lifts me.

> Yes, I accompany him to places

becomes

> Yes, I companion him to places
> Where the shy hares show their faces

becomes

> Where the shy hares print long paces.

On the other hand, he did his best to smooth an unsatisfactory ending to the poem:

> And if it be that at night I am stronger,
>   Go, too, by day I do:
> Please, then, keep him in gloom no longer,
>   Even ghosts tend thereto!

by an usually thorough re-writing:

> Tell him a faithful one is doing
> All that love can do
> Still that his path may be worth pursuing,
> And to bring peace thereto.

5

Hardy's later verse, i.e. that published in the 1920s, in his last three volumes, seems to me to show a gradual decline, though it should be remembered that it is relative only. The poems in *Winter Words*, for instance, are competent at the worst, and at best a great deal more. Much of the tension, however, seems to have gone; if these volumes have fewer of his vices, they lack many of his virtues too. When the immediate effects of Emma's death wore off, Hardy's poetry changed. Predictably, the important changes are those in subject-matter. 'Philosophy' tends to be expounded less; he had worked this vein extensively in *The Dynasts*. The meditative, pondering poems, which are allied to them in inspiration and which frequently show Hardy at his best, become rarer too. The odd stories and the songs continue unabated; unfortunately, since it needs a rather special taste to appreciate many of these.

The most obvious innovation in subject, however, is the steep rise in the quantity of description. Blunden notices this, observing also that 'some part of a view of life' is implied (p. 263). There is no point in attempting to provide statistics, since Hardy frequently draws some non-descriptive conclusion or moral and it is difficult to get agreement as to whether the poem is basically descriptive or not. Nevertheless, there are obvious changes. Apart from some triolets in

Poems of the Past and the Present, it is not until *Satires of Circumstance* that we meet poems having a high proportion of description (e.g. 'Before and After Summer'). In this volume and *Moments of Vision*, sometimes a point is made on the basis of a description (for instance 'On Sturminster Footbridge').

In *Late Lyrics and Earlier*, the first poem, 'Weathers', symbolizes an increase in the process; but it is the next volume, *Human Shows*, where description comes into its own, e.g. 'Bird Scene at a Rural Dwelling', 'Last Week in October', 'The Late Autumn', 'A Spellbound Palace', 'Night Time in Mid-Fall', 'A Sheep Fair', 'Snow in the Suburbs', 'Nobody Comes', 'Last Look Round St Martin's Fair', and so on. This is continued in *Winter Words*. These poems are often excellent examples of their genre; but it is significant that Hardy in his earlier period rarely produced them. Verbal eccentricities are rare here; Hardy's descriptive poems are not usually the product of the tensions which produced his best work.

Something of the change can be seen by comparing 'The Temporary the All' with 'Best Times'. The themes are similar and as the latter, published in 1922, is described as 're-written from an old draft', the gap in time between the first inspiration of the poems may be much less than the dates of publication indicate.

At first sight the advantages are all in favour of 'Best Times'; it is obviously personal in inspiration and from a cluster of memories which produced a great deal of fine work; the metrical structure is competent, and the verbal mixture, seen so strongly in 'The Temporary the All', is lacking. It is indeed a very efficient poem, which seems to say exactly what its author intended. Most people will prefer it and it is difficult to fault their preference. To me, however, despite its personal origin, the poem seems curiously cold and off-hand, almost impersonal, which may be valuable in some poets' work, but not in Hardy's. Part of the trouble is that the poem is too smooth; the language, for Hardy, too obviously consistent. No one is likely to prefer 'The Temporary the All' on the first reading; later readings may make judgement harder, and I believe this to be so of a number of poems. Poetically, Hardy thrived on difficulties and one of the consequences of his development was that competence seemed to overcome them too easily. We have seen that verbal idiosyncrasies were frequently removed from *Wessex Poems*; too often, later, they seem not to have manifested themselves at all.

Development sometimes seems to be used as a kind of shibboleth; there is an assumption, often tacit, that a poet who does not pass through discernible stages in some way fails in a vital part of his craft. (He certainly gives the commentators less to write about.) There is no need for a critic of Hardy to dispute this point, since it is obvious that a poet who begins publication and serious production in his late fifties cannot be classed with those who start in youth or even adolescence. In any case, Hardy was himself from the start; the existence of strong influences from other poets should not be allowed to disguise this, but I think I have demonstrated that there was *some* development and that it was genuine and not superficial, since it affected almost everything; form, ideas and language.

IX

Conclusion

THE starting point of this investigation was the sharp critical disagreement about Hardy's poetry and its somewhat anomalous standing in general esteem. The two problems are, to a large extent, one. The 'local' differences of opinion concerning poems play a large part in creating the peculiar repute of the poetry as a whole and are in turn affected by it. The typical symptom of this is the tone of grudging admiration which seems to be the prevailing attitude; this it is, I think, which is responsible for both the insistence on emphasizing the amount of inferior work and for the small number of poems which the critic really approves of. It seems that the critics are attracted against what they feel to be their judgement, perhaps against their will—certainly against their principles.

It would be an impossible task to describe, even in outline, the critical orthodoxies of the last forty years. Practically any statement can be contradicted, with references, and many potent attitudes are difficult to pin down at all. Miss Helen Gardner gives an example of this in her Introduction to a collection of essays on John Donne.[1] Remembering 'the years *entre deux guerres* during which Donne enjoyed a higher reputation and a greater popularity than at any time since the thirty years following the first publication of his poems' and that Donne was regarded as providing a 'norm' of

[1] *John Donne* (Englewood Cliffs, New Jersey, 1962), p. 1.

excellence in English poetry, she confesses her surprise 'at the difficulty of finding any essay in which this view is argued rather than taken for granted or opposed', or even 'essays which will sum up the intense enthusiasm for Donne's poetry which the young of both sexes felt in the Twenties and Thirties of this century'. She in fact failed 'to discover a worthy written monument of what memory tells me was a prevailing and "orthodox" view'. Attempts to lay bare more general and vaguer attitudes are almost certain to have even less success. All the same, like Miss Gardner, we know that there have been, and to some extent still are, such attitudes and that these are very powerful. It is the contention of this study that the peculiar reputation of Hardy as a poet is due partly to the action of certain attitudes and assumptions. Many of these have been considered earlier, but may be incorporated here in a rough summary.

In some quarters there has been a hostility to the presence of explicit ideas in poetry ('preaching' is the usual label) and they do exist in Hardy in sufficient quantity to give him a bad reputation. To this group is added the people who object to these particular ideas or allow themselves to be influenced by hostility, even if they do not formally object to them. One of the few critical views of T. S. Eliot which did not soften towards the end of his life was his dislike of Hardy. 'When an author's mind is so antipathetic to my own as was that of Thomas Hardy, I wonder whether it might not have been better never to have written about him at all.'[1] Finally, when he read some of the accounts of his philosophy Hardy must have muttered: 'God protect me from my friends . . .'; his reputation as a 'thinker' has not been good for his reputation as a poet.

[1] *To Criticize the Critic and other Writings* (London, 1965), p. 24.

For much of this century the doctrine of organic or expressive form has been a potent and pervasive influence. Hardy was basically a 'formalist' and occasionally committed the 'crime' of contorting his verse to fit into prescribed and preordained patterns. This was made worse by his possession of a vague reputation as an innovator, which was found on closer inspection to be hollow. Allied to this was a claim, similarly exposed as largely sham, to be a dramatic poet, when powerful critical voices (Eliot, for instance) were holding that practically all great poetry was dramatic.

Hardy believed that 'the whole secret of a living style and the difference between it and a dead style, lies in not having too much style—being, in fact, a little careless, or rather seeming to be, here and there' (*Early Life*, p. 138). Minor faults are common enough to make it look as if he put this doctrine into practice and this offends readers and critics in an age of close reading, analysis, and a general rise in technical standards of poetry. (It is, I think, certainly true that the *average* level of competence is much higher than it was throughout Hardy's own life-time.) Randall Jarrell points out that technical competence, difficult enough to achieve, does not itself carry an author very far in critical repute, but is demanded as a *sine qua non* and any author appearing to lack it has a hard time.

Hardy's verse stands up to close scrutiny reasonably well; many of the weaknesses of vocabulary, rhythm, structure and so on exist only in the critic's understanding—or through a lack of it. I have emphasized that care and sympathy will remove many stumbling blocks. But close analysis is often only a partially effective instrument for dealing with many of these poems. One of the marks of this technique in the hands of its less able practitioners is a tendency to concentrate

P

on one thing at a time; this makes it an effective method for determining the virtues and defects of vocabulary *or* rhythm *or* structure *or* ideas. But this very virtue often makes it much more difficult to respond to the poem as a unity, and the peculiar value of Hardy's best poetry lies in its pre-eminent possession of this unity (all good poetry has it, but other poets frequently have *local* strengths which are often lacking in Hardy).

I am convinced that the source of this unity in Hardy's poems is the personality which most poems disclose; many of the poems *are* unities, they *are* integrated because they have this common link or, rather, are expressions of it. Concentration on particular aspects can remove difficulties and misunderstandings; it does little, through its very nature, to help the reader to approach the central core since this is personal and indivisible. It is, of course, essential to avoid the error of identifying this poetic personality with that of the man Hardy. The difference between the two has been plain to many observers and critics, including Siegfried Sassoon, whose poem 'At Max Gate' is based on this contrast:

> Old Mr Hardy, upright in his chair,
> Courteous to visiting acquaintance chatted
> With unaloof alertness while he patted
> The sheepdog whose society he preferred.
> He wore an air of never having heard
> That there was much that needed putting right.
> Hardy, the Wessex wizard, wasn't there.
> Good care was taken to keep him out of sight.
>
> Head propped on hand, he sat with me alone,
> Silent the log fire flickering on his face.

Here was the seer whose words the world had known.
Someone had taken Mr Hardy's place.[1]

One personality has obviously been formed by the other, it
is true; as is the fact that clues which help appreciation can be
found in Hardy's life. But constant critical 'sieving' is needed;
much biographical detail is irrelevant, or worse. (The recent
flood of gossipy pamphlets about Hardy from The Toucan
Press, now (1968) numbering about thirty-five is, despite
occasional items of interest, an outstanding example of the
unfortunate consequences of regarding all facts or alleged
facts as worth consideration.) The poetic personality is the
real source and centre and it exists only in the work. If, for
any reason, the reader does not respond to this personality,
then he will respond only to those poems which meet the
critical criteria he brings with him; and, as we have seen, the
number can be very small.

Critical theories about the necessary impersonality or
poetry are likely to be a handicap when Hardy is being
considered, and the inventor, or modern reviver, of the
theory, T. S. Eliot, logically enough picked on Hardy as one
of the outstanding examples of personality in modern
literature. Admittedly, he considers only one example, a
minor piece of prose, but the instinct was right. M. H.
Abrams, discussing critical theories, describes various pro-
cedures, one of which 'analyses it [the work] as a self-
sufficient entity constituted by its parts in their internal
relations, and sets out to judge it solely by criteria intrinsic to
its own mode of being'. He adds that 'In America, at least,
some form of the objective point of view has already gone
far to displace its rivals as the reigning mode of literary

[1] *Collected Poems* 1908–1956 (London, 1961), p. 263.

criticism'.[1] There is, of course, ample room for discussion as to how far the rigor of the principles remains unqualified in practice, and also for pointing out, in Hardy's case, that the persona is largely *in* the poem; but it is hard to believe that a critic will feel happy with much of the verse *and* with such a critical theory. He may admire, but there will be some discomfort in his admiration and he would not be an 'objective' critic if he did not try to locate the cause of this discomfort inside the poem itself.

A large proportion of influential criticism has always been written by poets and it is probable that the proportion today is higher than ever before. It is notorious that they tend to judge literature in terms of the needs and pressures of their own work; among other things, they usually discuss writers whose influence, by attraction or repulsion, they feel. Put crudely, this means that there is a tendency to assess the importance of writers by their influences; creative writers may be polite and even cordial about poets remote from their own interests, but are apt to betray their fundamentally apathetic attitude by their failure to do anything more. Hardy's peculiar situation here was discussed at the beginning of this study. It would be easy to compile a long list of poets paying tribute to Hardy, but the critical harvest is very sparse (the chief item, Blunden's book, was commissioned by Hardy's publishers, partly as a centenary tribute). Several critics, for instance, Grigson and Furbank, claim that Hardy influenced many poets. 'Hardy's direct influence on the twentieth-century English poets has probably been greater than that of anyone save Eliot and Pound....'[2] No one, however, seems willing to give details or even ask some

[1] *The Mirror and the Lamp*, pp. 26, 28.
[2] P. N. Furbank, *Selected Poems of Thomas Hardy* (London, 1964), p. xxii.

obvious questions. For instance, Pound who says that Hardy taught him something does not show very obviously what it was (since it is hard to believe that he needed to learn the importance of subject-matter from Hardy) and Graves, while recommending Hardy to young poets, has apparently kept to other paths himself.

Scattered examples of influence are, it is true, easy enough to find, though they usually come from a poet's very early work (W. H. Auden for example). As instances at opposite extremes, consider a complete poem 'Geometry' by John Crowe Ransom from *Poems about God* (1919) and a few lines from Blunden's early poem 'Festubert: the old German Line':

> One derelict grim skeleton
> That drench and dry had battened on
> Still seemed to wish us malison.

It is also true that close imitation, amounting to pastiche, can be found; see, for example, de la Mare's 'Thomas Hardy' and C. Day Lewis's 'Singing Children: Lucca della Robbia' (from *An Italian Visit*); the latter, in particular, seems a Hardy poem that, by some accident, Hardy forgot to write. Furthermore, no lover of parody should miss William Plomer's 'A Right of Way: 1865', which begins

> Decades behind me
> When courting took more time,
> In Tuphampton ewe-lease I mind me
> Two trudging aforetime:
> A botanist he, in quest of a sought-after fleabane,
> Wheedling his leman with 'Do you love *me*, Jane?'

Most of these resemblances, of varied strength and serious-ness, have one thing in common; they imitate him where he is most imitable, usually in idiosyncrasies of vocabulary and rhythm. It should be fairly obvious, however, that for another poet to be *seriously* influenced by Hardy is rather unlikely, because as the real Hardy, the one who is worth being influenced by, started from subject, the poet being influenced would do the same. He might well take over, or rather perceive anew, Hardy's subject-matter, but since he would be attempting to render *his* perception it is not likely that he would employ Hardy's peculiarities of vocabulary.

This conclusion, which is attainable on purely theoretical grounds, was made clear to me partly by accident. I read the poems by Philip Larkin in *The New Poetry*[1] and noted that no less than six of the eight poems, though not like Hardy, dealt with Hardy themes ('Wedding Wind', 'If, My Darling', 'Going', 'Wants', 'The Whitsun Weddings', 'Mr Bleaney'). Two days later I read a review by Larkin of Emma Hardy's *Some Recollections*, in which his understanding of Hardy is made quite evident.[2] Another interesting though less important example is seen in a few of the poems of John Betjeman. There is much more of Hardy in such poems as 'Portrait of a Deaf Man' and 'I. M. Walter Ramsden' than in 'Dorset', Betjeman's rather brassy travesty of Hardy's 'Friends Beyond'. The possibility of genuine influence seems proved therefore, but such cases must be rare.

2

It is clear that besides the differences in valuation which always exist between critics, there are others which have

[1] Ed. A. Alvarez (Harmondsworth, 1962).

[2] *Critical Quarterly*, iv (1962), 75–9. Later Larkin gave something of his poetic history with regard to Hardy in the Preface to the second edition of *The North Ship* (London, 1966), p. 10.

arisen because Hardy has managed to cut across a number of critical orthodoxies at the same time and because appreciation frequently makes progress slowly against theoretical opposition (which need not always manifest itself in theoretical terms). This, I think, explains the fact, noted by Hynes, that there seems to be a 'radical disagreement between the professional critics and cultivated taste' (p. 13). He remarks 'the New Critics, though they have not given Hardy much attention, have treated his poems with sympathy and understanding when they have dealt with them at all'; though without, apparently, considering the probability that a failure of enthusiasm is very likely when natural inclinations and theoretical assumptions conflict.

If, when, and how, this situation will change is hard to say. Critical theories are made, and unmade, by critical theoreticians and doubtless the perpetual flux of opinion which has loosened many of the orthodoxies discussed above will continue its work; Hardy will be a beneficiary of this, as the cluster of assumptions which dominated critical thinking until recently are such that almost any change is to his advantage. There are signs that a *general* change is in full swing. A recently published volume[1] contains interviews with forty-five poets with birth-dates stretching from 1893 to 1931. Obviously no conclusions can be more than tentative, but it is fairly clear that the reign of organic form is over theoretically as well as in practice. Virtually every poet advocates strict forms (only the eldest contributor, Sir Herbert Read, and the solitary American, Sylvia Plath, support some kind of free verse). It is also interesting that three of the contributors seem to have as their own subject matter the related theme of love and death which Hardy has.

[1] *The Poet Speaks* (London, 1966), ed. Peter Orr.

Where Hardy's poetry is concerned, however, it is easy to exaggerate the change. The long delay in the completion of this book has caused me to think more than once that it had been overtaken by events and belonged to a bygone critical context, especially when it is claimed that Hardy is becoming a fashionable poet. But things have changed less than appears on the surface. The old attitudes, though perhaps a little less rigid, seem very deep rooted. The authors of three books on Hardy published in the last four years, George Wing (1963), R. C. Carpenter (1964) and Roy Morrell (1965), agree in emphasizing the novels, and two of them, Carpenter and Morrell, hold the traditional 'we need bother with only a score of the poems' view, the latter admittedly with some qualification.

Although the theories and assumptions which constitute Hardy's 'philosophy' are still alive, they are also to some extent 'historical' and will become increasingly so. They will, therefore, lose much of their power to irritate, but also their full and immediate impact on the mind and spirit. His readers will have to rely increasingly upon notes, commentators and background reading, and so he will come to the public on the same footing as his great predecessors whose work and reputation have overcome similar obstacles. He will, of course, always have some readers whose contact with his work is a kind of naked encounter, creating sympathy and comprehension without the need for intermediaries. It seems likely, too, that in the future, as in the past, their number will be increased in times of stress. The First World War was one such period when Hardy's stock rose and there was a similar, if less marked, movement during the Second.

Q. D. Leavis, after quoting a statement that only a

disenchanted sophomore could be impressed by Hardy's view of Life, admits that there is always a generation of such readers.[1] She refers to E. L. Woodward's *Short Journey* as an instance; an interesting one as it happens, since in it he not only mentions his great fondness for Hardy's novels and poems, but shows his awareness of what he calls 'the literature of destruction'.

Conversely there will always be readers whose temperaments will clash with Hardy's. Any kind of self-satisfaction is likely to produce this, the situation then being as he described it in 'In Tenebris II'. Furthermore, despite his reputation for intrusive and repeated expression of ideas, the true Hardy is a poet of the intimate whisper; and it is very easy for some people to get the tone wrong. Take, for example, the poem, 'Waiting Both'; Blunden after quoting it comments finely:

Only that. It does not ask for much in the margin. It confronts us like a lonely bridge in a fen, or the eye of a bird on a nest. It is a biography of all that is made, and yet it is Thomas Hardy, his alone. The question of the beautiful or significant hardly seems to arise. (p. 258)

I find myself completely in agreement; but I first read this poem, many years ago, in an anthology of humour where it appears with limericks on each side of it! This atrocity was committed about the same time as Blunden wrote the comment above. It seems unlikely that any amount of exhortation or explanation will do anything here.

The problems of repetitiveness and inferior work are difficult. The 'dross' seems unlikely to disappear in the near future and, in view of the present uncertainty of judgement,

[1] *Scrutiny*, xi (1943), 235.

it would be unwise to attempt to hasten the process. But the general reader has to be catered for, and is probably more important than the professional critics, or 'licensed tasters', as Hardy called them. The best approach for them appears to be by way of a book of selections, though it is impossible to recommend any existing volume without considerable reservation.

There are, in addition to the danger inseparable from *any* anthologizing, two approaches which must be avoided by any editor of Hardy's verse: the 'cross-section' and the 'jewels from rubbish-heaps'.

The first sounds plausible, especially when advocated in the cause of honesty, since it is claimed that in this way we have the verse as it really is, warts and all. But Hardy's verse is already inextricably various; nearly every poem has its quota of dross, even if it is dross transmuted temporarily to gold, and there is no need to display more of it. In any case the deliberate republication and dissemination of inferior verse is a heavy responsibility for an editor to shoulder. Such material should be allowed to lie dormant in its author's collected works.

On the other hand, the editor who sees himself as a dauntless prospector sieving malodorous heaps for a few nuggets is a danger too. Critical uncertainty is so marked at present that it is doubtful whether a satisfactory short selection is possible at all; too many serious candidates would be left out. (John Crowe Ransom, whose selection from Hardy is probably the best yet made, has commented on the unlikelihood of one Hardy anthologizer agreeing with another and on the quantity of good work waiting to be discovered.) Furthermore, one poem often throws light upon another if only by contrast. Lastly, and most importantly, Hardy should be read, if not complete, at any rate in bulk; there is a large quantity of verse, both relatively and absolutely which needs to be read sympathetically and with the understanding gained by reading the better work, which is similar to it in essence anyway. It is common knowledge that his verse grows on the reader, but there is less chance of this happening if the cream—assuming it can be identified— is to be strained off into a 'recognized' anthology.

Ultimately, however, the reader who is trying to enjoy what Hardy has to offer will have to make the effort which has been suggested several times in this study, to see the poems as the poetic unity that many of them are, to be in contact with the poetic persona revealed there. If Hardy seems a little tentative, clumsy or indiscriminate, they should remember the remark of Joubert: 'Those who have no thought beyond their words, and no vision beyond their thoughts, have a very decisive style'; and also that of R. P. Blackmur about Hardy's personal rhythm. 'Once it has been struck out in the open, it is felt as ever present, not alone in his thirty or forty finest poems but almost every- where in his work.'

It is a truism that great literature is in the last resort ineffable; Pound must have felt this when he was discussing Hardy: 'Given those specifications, poem after poem of Hardy's leaves one with nowt more to say. Expression co- terminous with matter: Nothing for disciples' exploitation.'[1]

All this can be seen in, for instance, 'Proud Songsters'; the personal rhythm, expression coterminous with matter, the lack of anything for disciples' exploitation; all ensuring that there is 'nowt more' to say, that an attempt to say anything would be impertinence or anti-climax.

[1] *Guide to Kulchur* (London, 1938), p. 285.

The thrushes sing as the sun is going,
  And the finches whistle in ones and pairs,
And as it gets dark loud nightingales
   In bushes
Pipe, as they can when April wears,
  As if all Time were theirs.

These are brand-new birds of twelve-months' growing,
Which a year ago, or less than twain,
No finches were, nor nightingales,
   Nor thrushes,
But only particles of grain,
  And earth, and air, and rain.

      (*Collected Poems*, pp. 797–8)

The Question of Influences

He went his own way, respecting the performances of others, but never in the least influenced by them or eager to compete with them. (C. M. Bowra)

Influence-spotters don't have a very happy time with him. (C. Day Lewis)

These extracts seem to represent the general opinion of Hardy's relations with his predecessors and contemporaries; critical attitudes to Hardy being what they are, it is of course over-optimistic to expect that it would be the only voice heard.

Few poets have learnt from other poets more expertly than Hardy, with such a flair for what to take and what to leave in order to strengthen the original personal gift. (Douglas Brown)

The freedom-from-influence view is inherently improbable taken at its face value; even when interpreted loosely, it still cannot apply to many poets. The literary 'kinless loon' must be very rare indeed, and very reasonably so, for as Ben Jonson remarked 'he that was only taught by himself had a fool to his master'. Furthermore the evidence seems to tell against this view. Many influences can be seen, some considerable and diffused through large areas of his verse; others minor and limited; while yet others are trivial. Many of them are the deposit left by an extensive reading of verse, of which the two-year period mentioned earlier (p. 147) is the most concentrated part.

The influence of William Barnes has been referred to already. It should be remembered that, as they were personally known to each other when Hardy was very young, Barnes would have all the prestige which early and personal association can give; furthermore this early acquaintance ensures that there is no 'pre-Barnesian' work. Apart from strengthening any tendencies which Hardy might have had towards the use of local language and incident, Barnes's influence can be seen mainly in structure; that he was a considerable influence has never been doubted.

Hardy considered Browning to be the greatest Victorian poet and his influence can be seen working in several ways, notably in the handling of a mixed vocabulary and, possibly, the penchant for the 'dramatic' form; (Browning's 'so many utterances of so many imaginary persons, not mine', could easily have been the source of similar remarks by Hardy). 'Panthera' and 'In the Servants' Quarters' are 'Browning' poems in a way that most of the rest of Hardy's verse is not. In addition there are many examples of more restricted influence. Thus Blunden points out that Hardy's 'To Outer Nature' relies on Browning's 'A Pretty Woman'. (The poem's use of the rare 'sempiternal' and 'hodiernal' in the last stanza are paralleled in the 'hodiern, modern, sempitern', of Dunbar's 'Ane Ballat of our Lady'). C. Day Lewis himself recommends the reader to compare certain stanzas of Browning's 'By the Fireside' with the first sixteen lines of Hardy's 'Under the Waterfall' (McDowall had already noticed the 'Browningesque' quality of this poem). The lines 'we were mixed at last in spite of the mortal screen' are very like Hardy. 'The Seasons of Her Year' is based on a similar idea to Browning's 'Three Days'. But probably Browning's greatest legacy to Hardy was something less ponderable; it is hard to believe that his successful dealing with linguistic mixtures, his taste for the grotesque, his line of rough-textured verse did not serve as both example and precedent.

Tennyson, as might be expected, seems to have had little interest for Hardy; the chief influence is towards parody. Hardy uses the 'In Memoriam' stanza to arrive at very different conclusions in 'A Sign Seeker' and similar links connect Hardy's 'Amabel' with 'Claribel' and 'Oriana'. The echo of 'Mariana' in 'An Ancient to Ancients', which Furbank sees, is likely enough since Tennyson is mentioned in the poem. One of Hardy's titles, *Time's Laughingstocks*, comes from *The Princess* ('The drunkard's football, laughing-stocks of Time').

The third great Victorian poet, Arnold, was an acquaintance of Hardy. They had a melancholy streak in common, so some resemblances may be due to this and not to direct influence. Arnold certainly anticipated one of Hardy's habits, that of using two visitings of the same scene as a peg for a statement about Mutability or a meditation upon it. Compare, for instance, 'Resignation', 'Thyrsis' and perhaps, 'A Summer Night' with Hardy's 'An Anniversary' and 'The Second Visit'). Arnold's 'To a Gypsy Child' parallels in idea several poems, particularly 'To An Unborn Pauper Child'. Many of the meditative parts of 'Stanzas from the Grande Chartreuse' are Hardyan, for example:

> My melancholy, sciolists vow,
> Is a pass'd mode, an outworn theme—
> As if the world had ever had
> A faith, or sciolists been sad!

> ...We admire with awe
> The exulting thunder of your race;
> You give the universe your law,
> You triumph over time and space!
> Your pride of life, your tireless powers
> We laud them, but they are not ours.

These lines cover very similar ground to Hardy's 'The Impercipient' and 'In Tenebris II'. On one occasion only does influence seem probable rather than possible; 'Poor Matthias' is surely the original of Hardy's 'Last Words to a Dumb Friend'.

Wordsworth is, of course, a strong influence but difficult to be specific about, since Hardy, quite apart from parallelisms and common influences (for instance ballads) has digested his work well. But 'Ruth' has contributed something, I think, to 'The Dance at the Phoenix', and 'The Sailor's Mother' to 'The Love Letters'. Hardy himself pointed out Wordsworth's influence on 'The Widow Betrothed' ('. . . it must have been written after I had read Wordsworth's famous Preface to Lyrical Ballads, which influenced me much, and influences the style of the poem, as you can see for yourself.' Letter to Gosse, 18 Feb. 1918. Quoted in Purdy, p. 113).

Housman's 'Is My Team Ploughing?' seems to have been the inspiration of Hardy's 'Ah, are you Digging on my Grave?' There are other resemblances, but if these are anything more than coincidence they are probably due to common influences such as Heine who was one of Housman's models and whose 'Ich stand in dunkeln Träumen' Hardy translated (as 'Song from Heine', *Collected Poems*, p. 167). 'The Comet at Yell'ham' (see above, p. 107), for instance, certainly seems like Heine, and a little like Housman.

The Greek tragedians, early, persistent and considerable

influences, affected ideas more than anything else. Hardy was in ,the habit of using them as precedents when he was accused of excessive pessimism. Horace was his favourite Latin poet, as he had been Wordsworth's. Horace's Sapphics may have had something to do with Hardy's fondness for a short final line in a stanza; found, to take poems near to each other, in 'Weathers', 'The Maid of Keinton Mandeville', 'Epeisodia', 'Faintheart in a Railway Train' and 'At Moonrise and Onwards'. He also seems to have been impressed by Horace's exhortation against rushing into print (*Early Life*, p. 64).

In addition, one can find occasional traces of inspiration from miscellaneous sources; the echoes of Campbell and Hunt noted by Blunden (pp. 257, 260), and of Hood ('Afternoon Service at Mellstock' from 'I remember, I remember', and 'Silences' from Hood's 'Silence'). There are a few more, and doubtless yet others have escaped notice.

Thus, it may seem that here we have a rather derivative poet with little style of his own; all the more so, as his influences are so miscellaneous. In fact some of these are unimportant by any standards and others are not what they seem to be. Thus, the influence of Barnes, probably the strongest of all, is really rather limited, being almost entirely technical. The use of dialect, vocabulary expanded by analogy, stanzaic forms, use of refrain; all these could have been, and in many cases no doubt were, taken over from Barnes. What one notices quickly, however, is that the two rarely seem to be interested in the same things or to look at things in the same way; and as we have seen the predominance of subject and personal vision is basic in Hardy. He was aware of the gulf between them.

His rustics are, as a rule, happy people, and very seldom feel the sting of the rest of modern mankind—the disproportion between the desire for serenity and the power of attaining it.[1]

Barnes was a sophisticated craftsman but a naive thinker. Linguistically and metrically he ranged the world; otherwise, he barely reached the boundaries of Dorset. The difference is partly chronological; a social, economic, scientific, literary, and theological revolution lay between them. In short, the characteristic nineteenth-century 'dialogue of the mind with itself' is lacking in Barnes; what interested Hardy, apart from a regretful sympathy with Barnes's view of the Dorset dialect, was the patience, skill and learning.

We find him warbling his native wood notes with a watchful eye on the predetermined score. (Preface to *Select Poems*, p. ix)

Something of the difference in tone and outlook between them can be seen by comparing Barnes's 'Vellèn the Tree' (*Select Poems*, p. 110) with Hardy's 'Throwing a Tree', as the subjects are close enough to make comparison fruitful. Barnes's poem, like Hardy's, is a lament but is set in a community; the tree had shaded mowers and haymakers: meals had been eaten under it. The felling is communal also, e.g. *we* took, *we* cut, *we* bent, *we* did run. The lament is for the disappearance of a convenient shelter and landmark.

Notice, in contrast, the beginning of Hardy's poem:

The two executioners stalk along the knoll.

There is no sense of community, merely two professionals doing a job coldly and efficiently. The process seems a more painful one, and is performed not by 'us', but Jack and Ike.

[1] 'The Rev. William Barnes, B.D.' in *Life and Art by Thomas Hardy*, collected by Ernest Brennecke Jr. (New York, 1925), p. 53.

Finally, when we have been absorbed in the details of execution the last line arrives with a shock:

And two hundred years' steady growth has been ended in less than two hours.

This introduces a dimension beyond Barnes's poem. It would, incidentally, be interesting to extend the comparison to include Cowper's 'The Poplar Field', Hopkins's 'Binsey Poplars' and Charlotte Mew's 'The Trees are Down' (the last is by a little known poet of whom Hardy thought highly).

Much the same is true of Browning; Hardy must have admired his linguistic energy, freedom and scope, but his optimism (as Hardy saw it at any rate) was a puzzle, his fondness for the remote in time and place would arouse little enthusiasm, and while Browning in some ways, at any rate, is genuinely dramatic, Hardy is not. 'Panthera' is the severest test; there obviously *is* a lot of Browning here (for example the use of blank verse; rare outside *The Dynasts*), but much that is not. It is not dramatic but reminiscent; not a process of thought being created but a story being told; not a character being shown, but a particular situation.

What holds for these two comparatively important influences holds *a fortiori* for the rest. Hardy obviously knows his Wordsworth and his ballads, but is different from them; as for the others, generally speaking the more obvious the influence is, the less important the poem.

The position is, therefore, that many influences can be detected in Hardy's work, but few are important and none are very strong. In his best poems, where the influences exist at all, they have been absorbed leaving little if any residue. Douglas Brown appears to be right then, in claiming Hardy to be a poet who digests his influences and in claiming that he knows what to take and what to leave. The last clause is important. Putting aside Barnes as a special case, Hardy's favourite poets seem to have been Shakespeare, Shelley, Browning and Swinburne (this judging by quotations used, critical comments and so forth). It is striking that except for the Shakespearian provenance of some early sonnets, only Browning's influence really shows in Hardy, and we have already seen how little it really amounts to. Consciously or not, he knew that his favourites were not the food his creative faculties needed.

Are Sir Maurice Bowra and Mr Day Lewis wrong therefore? Only in so far as their claims are likely to create a sense of shock in an unwary reader who, taking what they say as true to the letter, finds obvious traces of some other poet.

They are basically right because the real Hardy is like no one else. The sources, largely sources of technique, are ultimately unimportant because they have been absorbed and often transformed by the creative personality of the poet. What belonged to someone else is now part of him, and comes to the reader as such.

Hardy and Existentialism

Hardy's philosophy has been referred to fairly often in this study, but mainly to show how it formed the poet and his poetry. Apart from this, my chief purpose has been to insist that it is much more consistent and tenable than it is usually given credit for; not because of any wish to recommend the philosophy *outside* the poetry, but because lack of sympathy for its manifestations *inside* are likely to be severely disabling to any reader. No attempt has been made to connect Hardy with any later philosopher or philosophical movements although such a connection, or lack of it, affects the accept-ability of the poems to the modern reader. I believe that there is a connection, though I emphasize that the position taken up in this study does not depend upon any such connection being demonstrable or, indeed, existing at all.

If certain emotional attitudes found in Hardy's poems are considered: the feeling that Man is an alien in a Universe which is possibly hostile and certainly indifferent; the conviction that he will have to make sense of it himself if any sense is to be made at all; the necessity of taking up an attitude even though it may be logically groundless or almost certainly false; then the reader is likely to be reminded of one modern philosophy—Existentialism. This now seems fairly obvious, but I only became aware of it at a com-paratively late stage of the writing of this book; and then partly because I realized that the philosophers who helped me most to get the 'feel' of Hardy's thought, Kierkegaard and Unamuno, were also the ancestors of Existentialism.

Such a connection is not likely to have passed completely unnoticed and I discovered later that Mr Gilbert Neiman had already considered Hardy's position as an Existentialist. There is no point in discussing what has not only been done already but done well, so the interested reader should consult Mr Neiman's article, with its clinching references to de Beauvoir and Camus ('Thomas Hardy, Existentialist' in *Twentieth-Century Literature*, Vol. 1, No. 4, Jan. 1956, pp. 207–14).

The same conclusion can be reached by a different route. I have emphasized already the similarity between Hardy's thought and that of the Gnostics. (I have no evidence that Hardy knew anything of Gnosticism, apart from any scraps he might have picked up from Mill and Leslie Stephen, though his remark about popular religion being 'Manichaean in essence' is certainly significant.)

The greatest modern authority on Gnosticism is probably Professor Hans Jonas, and his book, *The Gnostic Religion* (2nd ed., Boston, 1963), is an interesting survey not only of Gnostic philosophy and literature, but of the temperament which finds them congenial. Again and again one finds passages which seem to 'chime' with Hardy:

The world is the work of lowly powers which though they may mediately be descended from Him do not know the true God and obstruct the knowledge of Him in the cosmos over which they rule (p. 42).

The Universe . . . is like a vast prison whose innermost dungeon is the earth, the scene of man's life (p. 43).

The immediately relevant point, however, is that Professor

Jonas, a disciple of Heidegger, became interested in Gnosticism through his knowledge of Existentialist philosophy and has found that they tend to elucidate each other. He emphasizes that the resemblances are the result of parallel situations, a similar spiritual crisis and cultural break-up.

The existence of an affinity or analogy across the ages, such as is here alleged, is not so surprising if we remember that in more than one respect the cultural situation in the Greco-Roman world of the first Christian centuries shows broad parallels with the modern situation. (pp. 325–6)

These parallels are discussed in the 'Epilogue: Gnosticism, Existentialism and Nihilism', to the second edition of *The Gnostic Religion*.

It is no part of my intention to go into the details of Hardy's Existentialist affiliations, but the connection between his thought and a philosophy which Jonas describes as 'conceptual, sophisticated and eminently "modern" in more than chronological sense' (p. 320) should be considered by anyone who feels inclined to write off Hardy's views as Victorian relics. The problem of how Man is to behave in a Universe which seems to have no values other than those Man can create himself is hardly a dead issue. Hardy would probably have shared the opinion of the Talmudic philosopher who considered whether the world ought to have been created. The conclusion was that it would have been much better if it had not, but since the damage was done, Man ought to devote himself to the doing of good deeds.

SELECT BIBLIOGRAPHY

The following list is limited to the books, apart from those of Hardy himself, which I used most in the writing of this study. This principle of selection was bound to produce gaps which I shall not attempt to defend except by saying that many other works were consulted and found useful, and that a different critical viewpoint would produce a different, but equally valid, list. London is the place of publication unless otherwise stated.

Archer, William, *Real Conversations* (1904)

Blackmur, R. P., *Language as Gesture* (1954)

Blunden, Edmund, *Thomas Hardy* (1941)

Brown, Douglas, *Thomas Hardy* (1954)

Coleridge, S. T., *Biographia Literaria*, ed. J. Shawcross (Oxford, 1907)

Collins, V. H., *Talks with Thomas Hardy at Max Gate, 1920–22* (1928)

Eliot, T. S., *The Three Voices of Poetry* (1953)

Guerard, Albert J. (ed.), *Thomas Hardy: A Collection of Critical Essays* (Englewood Cliffs, New Jersey 1963)

Hardy, Emma, *Some Recollections*, ed. Evelyn Hardy and Robert Gittings (1961)

Hardy, Florence Emily, *The Early Life of Thomas Hardy 1840–1891* (1928)

—, *The Later Years of Thomas Hardy 1891–1928* (1930)

Hardy, Evelyn, *Thomas Hardy; A critical biography* (1954)

Hardy, Evelyn (ed.), *Thomas Hardy's Notebooks* (1955)

Hickson, Elizabeth Cathcart, *The Versification of Thomas Hardy* (Philadelphia, 1931)

Hynes, Samuel, *The Pattern of Hardy's Poetry* (Chapel Hill, 1961)

Kierkegaard, Søren, *The Journals* (Oxford, 1938)

Leavis, F. R., *New Bearings in English Poetry* (New edn. 1950)

Lewis, Cecil Day, 'The Lyrical Poetry of Thomas Hardy' in *Proceedings of the British Academy* (1953)

McDowall, Arthur, *Thomas Hardy: A Critical Study* (1931)

Mill, John Stuart, *Three Essays on Religion* (1874)

Nowottny, Winifred, *The Language Poets Use* (1962)

Preyre, E. A., *The Freedom of Doubt* (1953)

Purdy, Richard Little, *Thomas Hardy: A Bibliographical Study* (1954)

Ransom, John Crowe (ed.), *Selected Poems of Thomas Hardy* (New York, 1961)

Richards, I. A., *Science and Poetry* (1926)

Rutland, W. R., *Thomas Hardy: A study of his writings and their background* (Oxford, 1938)

Southworth, James Granville, *The Poetry of Thomas Hardy* (New York, 1947)

Sutherland, James, *The Medium of Poetry* (1934)

de Unamuno, Miguel, *The Tragic Sense of Life* (1921)

Webster, Harvey Curtis, *On a Darkling Plain* (Chicago, 1947)

Young, G. M. (ed.) *Selected Poems of Thomas Hardy* (1940)

INDEX

89647

DATE DUE

821.89   1969   89647
H272Ma
AUTHOR

Marsden Kenneth
TITLE

The poems of Thomas Hardy...

DATE DUE	BORROWER'S NAME
RETURNED	GORDON Y 3
03 18 1	*Mark H. Earls* 3

821.89   1969
H272Ma
Marsden, Kenneth
The poems of Thomas Hardy...

OHIO DOMINICAN COLLEGE

LIBRARY

COLUMBUS, OHIO 43219

DEMCO